C K.
MBODIA

D1741627

Alexander Hamilton

A Scottish Sea Captain
in Southeast Asia
1689-1723

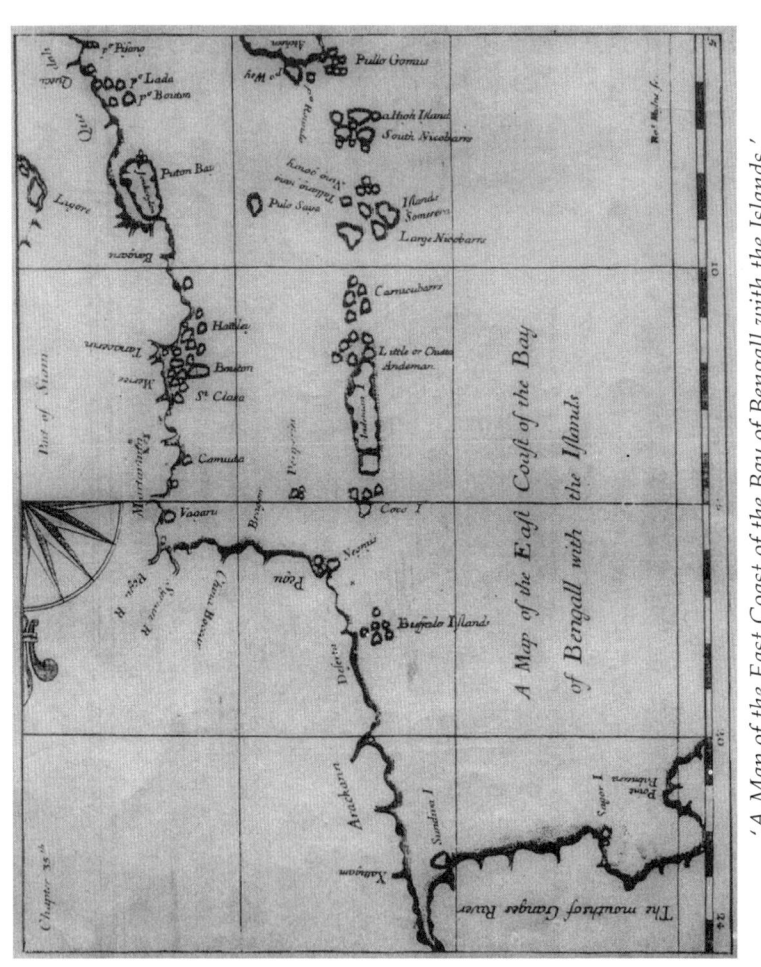

'A Map of the East Coast of the Bay of Bengall with the Islands.'

Alexander Hamilton

A Scottish Sea Captain
in Southeast Asia
1689-1723

edited by

Michael Smithies

SILKWORM BOOKS
Chiang Mai

Some other books by Michael Smithies
The Siamese Memoirs of Count Claude de Forbin 1685–1688
Abbé de Choisy: Journal of a Voyage to Siam, 1685–1686
A Thai Boyhood
Bight of Bangkok
Descriptions of Old Siam
Discovering Thailand (with Achille Clarac)
Old Bangkok
The Cultural Sites of Burma, Thailand, and Cambodia
(with Jacques Dumarçay)
The Discourses at Versailles of the First Siamese Ambassadors to France 1686–7
The Siamese Embassy to the Sun King:
The Personal Memoirs of Kosa Pan
Yogyakarta, Cultural Heart of Indonesia
A Javanese Boyhood
A Singapore Boyhood
A Busy Week: Tales of Today's Thailand

First published in 1997 by
Silkworm Books
54/1 Sridonchai Road, Chiang Mai 50100, Thailand.
E-mail: silkworm@pobox.com

Silkworm Books is a registered trade mark of
Trasvin Publications Limited Partnership.

Cover illustration: HMS Royal William built 1670 (The National Portrait Gallery)
Endpaper: The city of Lovek,
from F. Valentyn, *Oud en Nieuw Indien 1724-6*, Vol. 3.
Set in 11 pt. Palatino
Printed by O.S. Printing House, Bangkok.

CONTENTS

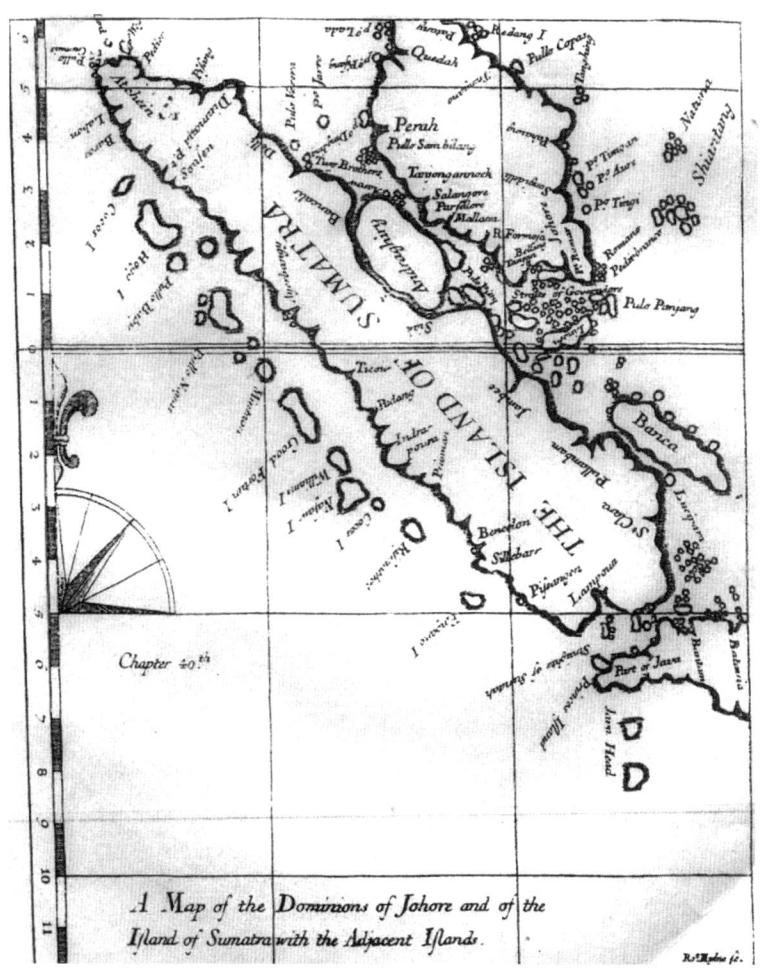

Chapter 40.th

A Map of the Dominions of Johore and of the
Island of Sumatra with the Adjacent Islands.

Ro.t Hydes fc.

'A Map of the Dominions of Johore and the Island
of Sumatra with the Adjacent Islands.'

PREFACE AND ACKNOWLEDGEMENTS

The desire to see in print again the work of 'our old navigator' has been with me for some time. Hamilton's book has only had four printings in nearly three centuries, the most recent being the excellent but unobtainable Argonaut Press edition published in 1930. This was ably edited by Sir William Foster, then President of the Society, and the present edition owes a great deal to the scholarship and insights found in his introduction and notes.

The limitation of this edition to Hamilton's account of Southeast Asia is one of practical necessity, for his original two volume work covers too great a geographical spread to be easily encompassed in a saleable volume today.

In addition to Sir William Foster, several other persons have contributed to elucidating points in the text. Thanks should be expressed to Professor G.D.E. Hall, whose *History of South-East Asia* has been, as always, of great assistance. Dr Clive Upton of the University of Sheffield, Professor Lee Kam Hing of Universiti Malaya, Ms Kanitha Kasina-Ubol at the Siam Society, and several others have helped enlighten me over particular details and given assistance in other ways. My gratitude goes to them, though none but myself is responsible for any errors that may be found here.

Michael Smithies

Bua Yai, Thailand
September 1995

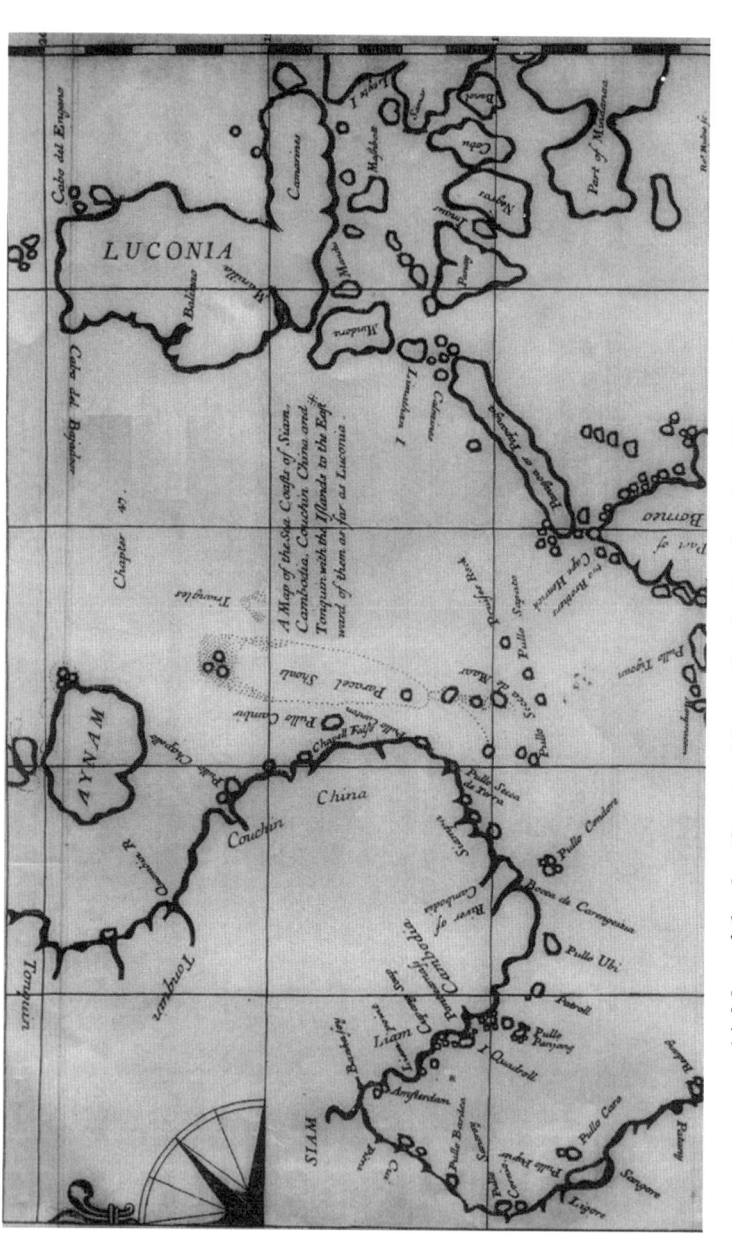

'A Map of the Sea Coasts of Siam, Cambodia, Couchin China and Tonquin with the Islands of the Eastward of them as far as Luconia.'

LIST OF ILLUSTRATIONS

A Scottish Sea Captain in Southeast Asia
1689-1723

A NEW
ACCOUNT
OF THE
Eaſt Indies,
BEING THE
OBSERVATIONS and REMARKS

Of Capt. ALEXANDER HAMILTON,

Who ſpent his Time there

From the Year 1688. to 1723. Trading
and Travelling, by Sea and Land, to
moſt of the Countries and Iſlands of
COMMERCE and NAVIGATION, between the Cape of *Good-hope,* and the
Iſland of *Japon.*

VOLUME I.

EDINBURGH,
Printed by *John Moſman* One of His MAJE-
STY's Printers, and ſold at the King's Prin-
ting-houſe in *Craig's* Cloſs. MDCCXXVII.

Title page of Volume I of first edition, Edinburgh 1727.

INTRODUCTION

Tantalizingly little is known about the details of Alexander Hamilton's life, and like the other British seafarer who recorded his travels in Southeast Asia later in the eighteenth century, Thomas Forrest, not even his date of birth or death are known for certainty. In Hamilton's preface to his only work, *A New Account of the East Indies*, first published in Edinburgh in 1727, he gives a few vague indications of his early life: "having a rambling mind, and a fortune too narrow to allow me to travel like a gentleman, I applied myself to the study of nautical affairs at Neptune's school, and, in the process of time, I came to be a Master of Arts in that university." Presumably born somewhere in Scotland, he must have gone to sea very young. While still in his youth, he travelled, he tells us, to "most of the maritime kingdoms of Europe, and some parts of Barbary. Then my curiosity led me to Jamaica, and then to the East Indies, where I spent between five and six and thirty years."

The purpose of his extended stay was honestly stated: "to get money". In this he was only modestly successful; he made plenty, but also lost a lot in his various business ventures, and when he finally retired to Scotland he had "enough to keep the meagre devil poverty from entering into my house", but no substantial fortune. He wrote up his recollections of his travels in retirement in Scotland, and "made a present of them to a particular friend" to print for "his own benefit and advantage".

Sir William Foster, in his introduction to the 1930 Argonaut Press edition of Hamilton's work (only the fourth to have appeared), has carefully plotted as much of Hamilton's life as can be deduced from what he tells us and from extant correspondence with the East India Company (EIC). He navigated freely across the Bay of Bengal and in the Far East, going backwards and forwards between the Red Sea, the Persian Gulf, to the spice islands and beyond to China at least four times, as trading opportunities arose. His carefully ordered account of the different countries visited, going from west to east, is in complete contrast with the toing and froing of his daily existence. Using Foster's information, one can establish a schema as follows:

16??	born in Scotland
16??	travelled along the coasts of Europe, North Africa and Jamaica
1688	left London on the *Shrewsbury* in April as "supernumerary sailor"
1689	arrived in Bombay in November
1690	went to Surat
1692?	to China
1693	in Amoy
1694	to Aceh and Malacca
1695	to Johor and then Surat 1696 in Bombay, to defend himself for his actions in Surat
1697	in Amoy again
1699	at Laharibandar, the port of Sind
1700	in Tatta, and then to China again, visiting Malacca en route

1702   in Aceh and Surat, then Johor and Malacca; hired a ship, the *Albemarle*, for trading from Surat

1703   his fourth journey to China, via Johor; was offered the island of Singapore by his friend the Sultan of Johor, which he refused as "of no use to a private person, though a proper place for a company to settle a colony on, lying in the centre of trade and being accommodated with good rivers and safe harbours"; thence to Macao

1704   from Macao to Johor, Surat, and Java in the *Vintaghurry*; in Batavia and Semarang, thence Goa and Surat

1705   to Bengal; from Calutta to Surat

1706   back to Calcutta for more trading

1707   in Cochin and Mahé, then Madras; loses a fortune in the burning of the English settlement at Benjarmasin in Borneo

1708   to Balasore and Calcutta again, where, short of funds, he mortgaged his house and sold a boat called the *Industry*

1709   his ship full of rice was seized by the French off the Andamans, but he bought from them a Dutch prize

1710   in Vizagapatam and Pegu

1711   in Madras from Pegu in the *Satisfactory*

1712   in Mokha on the Red Sea

1714   again in Mokha

1715   probably in the Persian Gulf

1716   once more in Mokha, in the *Morning Star*, and Bandar Abbas

1717   wounded in a pirate attack, but reached Bombay and Surat; appointed to command the East India Company's marine force at Bombay

1718	resigned his official post to "proceed on a voyage to Cambodia"; he went to Ayutthaya, the capital of Siam
1720	in Bombay, Cambodia, and Malacca
1721	in Bandar Abbas, Basra, and possibly Muscat
1722	in Bombay and Surat, where he sold the *Morning Star*
1723?	returned to Scotland
1724	in Holland on business
1725	in London, petitioning the Court of Directors of the EIC; back to Scotland (probably in or near Edinburgh) where he wrote his account during the "nights of two long winters"
1732	the *Gentleman's Magazine* records the death on 7 October of a "Capt. Alexander Hamilton", but this is not apparently referring to the author
1733	the Court Minutes of the EIC on 22 June record a petition of "Captain Alexander Hamilton... praying to succeed Captain Zachary Tovey" as the Company's surveyor of shipping
17??	died.

Omitted from this schema are the lengthy details concerning his different feuds and petitions which seem to have been the bread-and-butter of existence among seafarers of rank in the Orient at this period; the reader wishing to learn more of these details and of some of Hamilton's complex financial dealings should consult Foster's introduction.

Hamilton was clearly a fairly pugnacious character. As Foster notes, "he was hot-tempered and domineering, inclined to ride roughshod over everyone who stood in his way." He disliked ecclesiastics of whatever faith as much as he felt little empathy for the servants of the East India Company. He was quick to find fault and make enemies.

He disapproved of the Dutch and despised the Portuguese and the Spanish. Sometimes he speaks favourably of the inhabitants of the country his visits, but he also uses them whenever necessary.

He enjoys a good story, and incorporated several in his account; that of the poisoner Mistress Kennedy in Malacca stays long in the reader's memory. But much of his history has to be treated as no more than stories, often with little resemblance to fact. He gets dates and details wrong, most notably in his account of the ends of King Narai and Phaulkon in Lopburi. In his excuse, it must be said that he only recorded what he was told, and if the relation was inaccurate, he was none the wiser.

He was a clearly a good seaman, if only a marginally successful businessman. He could be resourceful and bold, as well as a generous friend. He was not without a sense of humour. He was, in short, hard-headed tough Scot who accepted the turns that fortune's wheel brought with equanimity.

Hamilton is one of the very few persons to have visited Siam in the eighteenth century and to have left an account of his stay (which was tempestuous and nearly ended in disaster for him); he gives interesting accounts of Malacca under the Dutch, Cambodia in its dark century, Pegu and Johor (that he was offered Singapore more than a century before it was taken by Raffles is a fascinating snippet). He is relatively brief in his record of Sumatra, Java, and the other islands now forming Indonesia, perhaps in part because he saw relatively little of them during his travels, and perhaps too because they were the subject of frequent comment by other voyagers.

Only two other editions exist of this text, apart from the first of 1727 and that of 1930 (both of which were published in two volumes). There was a reprint in London of 1744, published by Hitch and Millar (the Scot Millar was also the publisher of Samuel Johnson and Henry Fielding), and using the same plates as the first edition. John Pinkerton's *General Collection of the Best and Most Interesting Voyages*, published in London between 1808 and 1814, reproduced Hamilton's text in volume eight.

The first edition of Hamilton's text was dedicated to the premier duke of Scotland, his namesake Hamilton, in the hopes that "so illustrious a patron will be sufficient to protect and defend me" from the barbs of critics and others; he was clearly, in his preface, worried about the possible reception of his "little magazine". The rather wordy preface (in spite of his claim to "hate prolixity myself") gives some linguistic advice to other travellers in the East Indies. "One great misfortune that attends us European travellers in [greater] India is the want of knowledge of their languages, and they being so numerous". He points out that the Portuguese have "left a vestige of their language", and that this is the language most Europeans learn first, to speak to one another as well as to the peoples of the countries of the region.

The 1930 Argonaut Press edition of Hamilton had a facsimile of his only known letter, addressed to the Court of Directors of the East India Company and dated 30 July 1725, showing a legible hand and a clear signature without the usual flourishes of the time. No portrait of Hamilton is known to exist.

As in the late twentieth century there is a tendency to increased specialization of interest, this edition of Hamilton is limited to the chapters dealing with Southeast Asia (XXXVI-XLIX inclusive in the original edition). For ease of reading, spelling and punctuation have been modernized, but the syntax of the original kept.

The quality of the visuals in the 1727 edition leaves much to be desired. Hamilton's four maps of the region (apparently drawn by himself), require much turning around to read the locations marked, and while more detailed than many in respect of islands off the coasts, are altogether less satisfactory than, for example, Placide's well-known map of 1686 showing Chaumont's route through the Sunda Strait to Siam. Hamilton's two illustrations of Buddhist structures, of a Burmese pagoda and a Siamese temple, are even less satisfactory (indeed, the 'steeple' on the latter looks more like a minaret). Only the King of Siam's pleasure barge bears some apparent likeness, but is nowhere near as accurate or attractive in its representation as the many illustrations of royal barges found in Tachard (1687) and in La Loubère (1691).

This substantial extract from the second volume of Hamilton's account of the East Indies covering Southeast Asia in the early years of the eighteenth century is offered to the public in the hopes that it will stimulate and instruct, in the same fashion that Hamilton desired that "this my virgin essay will be civilly treated by the unprejudiced lovers of travels."

Michael Smithies

Bua Yai, Korat
April 1995

The audience hall of the Burmese kings, from Sir Henry Yule,
A Narrative of the Mission to the Court of Ava in 1855 *(1858)*

THE KINGDOMS OF PEGU
AND BURMA

G ives an account of the famous Kingdom of Pegu, its
situation and product[s], with its laws, customs, and
religion, and some historical accounts of their temples
and gods, of occurrences and revolutions in the state, and
how it became a province of the Kingdom of Burma

The sea coast from Negrais to Syriam Bar is in the
dominions of Pegu. There are some of the mouths of Pegu
River[1] [that] open on that coast into the sea. Dala is the first,
about fifty miles to the eastward of Negrais. China Backaar[2]
is another about forty miles to the eastward of Dala, and
between these openings there is a dangerous bank of black
sand, that runs four or five leagues[3] out into the sea, and so
far off there are but fourteen foot [of] water. About sixty
miles to the eastward of China Backaar is the bar of

---

[1]   'Pegu River... Dala... Negrais...' Hamilton in talking of the Pegu
      River is discussing the Irrawaddy, though his map marks the mouth
      of the Pegu River at that of the Sitang. Dala refers to the Kyondon
      mouth of the Irrawaddy. Negrais is an island considered in the 1750s
      a possible trading post of the East India Company (EIC), off the
      Irrawaddy delta.
[2]   China Backaar is now Thonkhwa.
[3]   A league was variable measure of distance, roughly 4 km.

Syriam[1], the only port now open for trade in all the Pegu dominions.

If by accident a ship bound to Syriam be driven a league or two to the eastward of that river's mouth, a strong tide carries her on hard sands till she sits fast on them, for anchors are of no use to stop them, because of the rapidity of the current; at low water the ships are dry when on those sands, and the sea leaves them, and retires five or six leagues, at which time the shipwrecked men walk on the sands toward the shore for their safety, for the sea comes back with so much noise, that the roaring of the billows may be heard ten miles off, for a body of waters comes rolling in on the sand, whose front is above two fathoms[2] high, and whatever body lies in its way it overturns, and no ship can evade its force, but in a moment is overturned; this violent bore the natives call a *macareo*.

About six leagues from the bar of Pegu River is the city of Syriam; it is built near the river's side on a rising ground, and walled round with a stone wall without mortar. The governor, who is generally of the blood royal, has his lodgings in it, but the suburbs are four times bigger than the city. It was many years in possession of the Portuguese, till by their insolence and pride they were obliged to quit it.

The ancient city of Pegu[3] stands about forty miles to the eastward of Syriam; the ditches that surrounded the city, which are now dry and bear good corn[4], testify that few cities in the world exceeded it in magnitude, for they are

[1] An important port, just below Dagon (Rangoon); Hamilton spells it throughout 'Syrian'. Philip de Brito, in the service of the King of Arakan, seized Syriam in 1599 and tried to gain control of all lower Burma; he was dislodged in 1613.

[2] A fathom is a measure of six feet (1.8288 metres).

[3] This is some 60 km north-east of modern Rangoon. Hamilton refers to its inhabitants as 'Peguers'; the modern form has been used here.

[4] Here, rice.

reckoned six or seven leagues round their outward polygon[1].

It was the seat of many great and puissant kings, who made as great a figure as any in the east, but now its glory is in the dust, for not one twentieth part of it is inhabited, and those are but the lower class of people who inhabit it. The cause of the ruin of the kingdoms of Pegu, Martaban[2], and some others under the dominions of Pegu, I had from some Peguans, in several discourses with them about that revolution, which was thus.

There was great love and friendship between the kings and subjects of Pegu and Siam, being next neighbours to one another, and they had a good intercourse of trade, both by land and sea, till in the fifteenth century, a Pegu vessel being at Odia[3], the chief city of Siam, and when ready to depart for Pegu, anchored one evening near a little temple a few miles below the city, and the master of the vessel, with some of his crew, going to worship in that temple, seeing a pretty well-carved image of the god Samsay[4], about a covet[5] high, fell in love with it, and finding his priests negligent in watching, stole him away, and carried him on board prisoner for Pegu. When the negligent priests missed their little god they were in a deplorable condition, lamenting their loss to all their neighbouring priests, who

---

[1] The many-sided outer defences of the city.
[2] Martaban, on the north bank of the Salween, was for a time the capital of the Mon kingdom, and was famous for its jars.
[3] Ayutthaya, the Siamese capital from 1351-1767; a description follows in Chapter Twelve. The inhabitants of Siam are usually called 'Siamers' by Hamilton; 'Siamese' has been preferred here.
[4] Hamilton either means Somana Khodom (Samana Gautama), the Buddha, or is referring to a corrupt form of *sasana*, meaning religion.
[5] A variant of 'cubit' (Portuguese *covado*), a measure varying from 18-22 inches, the length of the forearm. The *Oxford English Dictionary* cites Hamilton for 'covid', a variable Anglo-Indian linear measure.

advised them to complain to the King of Siam of the theft, which accordingly they did, imploring his good offices with the King of Pegu, to have their god sent back; and it happened that, by the unseasonable flood in the river that year, there came to be a great scarcity of corn, which calamity was imputed by the priests to the loss of Samsay, upon which the pious prince sent an embassy to his brother of Pegu desiring the restitution of the image, whose absence had caused so great loss and clamour in his country[1].

The King of Pegu, being as great a bigot as his brother of Siam, would by no means deliver back a god who had fled from the impieties of his native land to him for protection, and with that answer sent back the Siam ambassador, who was not a little mortified with the disappointment.

Since fair means could not persuade the Peguan [sic] to send back the little god, the Siamese was resolved to try what force would do, and accordingly raised an army of two or three hundred thousand men to invade the King of Pegu's dominions, and the first fury of the war fell on the province of Martaban, being contiguous to the territories of Siam, and with fire and sword destroyed the open country almost to the gates of the city of Martaban, where often the King of Pegu kept his court, and was formerly the metropolis of an independent kingdom, before Pegu reduced that country by conquest to be a province of theirs.

After the Siamese had satiated his cruelty and rage by the destruction of many poor innocents, he retired back to his own country very much elevated with pride and vainglory for his great achievements, but next year he was

---

[1] None of this seems to be based closely on the truth, like many of Hamilton's excursions into presumed history. Such disputes as there were, and they were frequent, between Pegu and Siam tended to be over white elephants rather than Buddha statues.

pretty well humbled, for the Peguan raised a much greater army, and embarking them in small boats on the River Menam[1] on which the city of Odia stands in one of its islands, his army was brought with so much celerity and secrecy that the Peguan brought the first news of his invasion, and pitching his tents round the city, soon brought it into great straits, by stopping the daily provisions that supported it; but unexpectedly the river bringing down great floods of water sooner than their ordinary time, the country about the city overflowed, and spoilt all the Peguan's provisions of corn, and drowned near the half of his army, which obliged him to raise the siege, and retire to his own dominions.

Next year, the Siamese, to be revenged, levied another great army, with which he overran all the inland countries of Pegu that lay near him, and annexed them to his own dominions. The Peguan, finding that he could not recover his lands without foreign aid and assistance, invited the Portuguese, whose name began to be dreadful in India, and by the great encouragement he gave them, got about 1,000 volunteers into his service. Neither the Siamese nor the Peguans at that time understood the use of firearms, and their noise and execution at so great a distance terrified them. With the Portuguese assistance, the Peguan went with his army, which was very numerous, to find out the Siamese, and having found him, gave him battle; the Portuguese, being in the front with their firearms, soon put the Siamese to flight before they could come to handy blows, on which he left the Peguan's country in greater haste than he came into it.

The King of Pegu was so sensible of the Portuguese service in gaining the battle and driving the Siamese out of

---

[1]   The Chao Phya River; Hamilton spells it 'Memnon'.

his conquered country that he made one Senhor Thoma Pereyra[1], who commanded the Portuguese in the war, generalissimo of all his forces, which preferment made the Portuguese so insolent that in a few years they became intolerable to all ranks and degrees of persons in Pegu.

Both kings grew tired of war, but both [were] too proud to make advances toward peace, so that for many years they had skirmishing with small parties, though no set battles, and wherever the Portuguese arms went, they had victory to accompany them.

The King of Pegu, to have his forces nearer the borders of Siam, settled his court at Martaban, and kept the Portuguese near him, to be ready on all occasions either to repel or assault the Siam forces, as opportunity served, and Thoma Pereyra was the darling favourite at court. He had his elephants of state, and a guard of his own countrymen to attend him. One day as he was coming from court in state on a large elephant towards his own palace, he chanced to hear music in a burgher's house, whose daughter, being a very beautiful virgin, had been married that morning to a young man of the neighbourhood. The general went to the house and wished them joy, and desired to see the bride. The parents took the general's visit for a great honour done them, and brought their daughter to his elephant's side; he being smitten with her beauty, ordered his guard to seize her and carry her to his house.

---

[1]   There seems to be a confusion here between Diogo Pereira, in Siamese service, and Diogo Suares de Albergaria, working for King Bayinnaung (r.1551-1581) who defeated the Mon forces outside Pegu. The story that follows seems to be condensed in its time sequence from the version in Mendes Pinto's *Peregrinaçam* (c.1575) Chapters 191-2. Diogo Suares was a pirate and a murderer who had to flee Goa for a time and rose to power under Tabinshwehti, brother-in-law of Bayinnaung.

14

account I had at Pegu in Anno 1709 both from Peguans and Portuguese, who agreed in the history as I have related it.

The dominions of Burma are at present very large, reaching from Mergui[1] near Tenasserim, to the province of Yunnan in China, about 800 miles from north to south, and 250 miles broad from west to east. It has no seaport but Syriam, and that river is capable to receive a ship of 600 tons. The town drives a good trade with Armenians[2], Portuguese, Moors[3] and Gentows[4], and some English; their import is several sorts of Indian goods, such as betelas, mulmuls, cossas, sannis, orangshays, tangebs[5], European hats coarse and fine, and silver. The customs are 8 $^1/_2$ per cent which, with other charges, amount to about 12 in the 100. The product of the country is timber for building, elephants, elephants' teeth[6], beeswax, stick-lac[7], iron, tin, oil of earth[8], wood oil[9], rubies the best in the world, diamonds, but they are small, and are only found in the craws[10] of poultry and pheasants, and one family has only the indulgence to sell them, and none dare open the ground to dig for them. Saltpetre they have in abundance, but it is death to export it, plenty of gansa[11] or lead, which passeth

[1]   As is indicated later, Mergui was Siamese.

[2]   There was a thriving Armenian trading community in Burma, Madras, and Ayutthaya in the late seventeenth century.

[3]   Arabs or Muslims rather than Moroccans.

[4]   Gentiles, heathen.

[5]   'betelas, mulmuls, coassas, sannis, orangshays, tangebs'. These are all different varieties of Indian and Persian textiles; 'betelas' were thin white Indian veils, and 'mulmuls' were more commonly known as muslins.

[6]   Ivory.

[7]   Lac in its natural state on twigs.

[8]   Petrol.

[9]   Gum.

[10]   Crops, or gullets.

[11]   A mixture of copper, tin and lead used in Pegu, Burma and Arakan for coins.

all over the Pegu dominions for money. About twenty sail of ships find their account in trade for the limited commodities, but the Armenians have got the monopoly of the rubies, which turns to a good account in their trade; and I have seen some blue sapphires there that I was told were found on some mountains of this country.

The country is very fruitful in corn, fruits, and roots, and excellent legumen of several species; abundance of wild game either quadrupeds or winged. In the months of September and October, wild deer are so plentiful that I have bought one for three or four pence; they are very fleshy, but no fat about them. They have many sorts of good fish, and swines' flesh and poultry are both plentiful and good.

They wear none of our European commodities but hats and ribbons, and the gentry will give extravagant prices for fine beaver hats, and rich ribbons flowered with silver and gold, and if it be never so broad it is stretched up the crown of the hat as far as it can go, and they use no sort of cock[1] to their hats. Cotton cloths from Bengal and Cormandel[2], with some striped silks, are best for their market, and silver of any sort is welcome to them. It [sic] pays the king 8 $1/_2$ per cent custom, but in lieu of that high duty, he indulges the merchants to melt it down, and put what alloy they please in it, and then to pass it off in payments as high as they can.

Rupee silver, which has no alloy in it, will bear 28 per cent of copper alloy, and keep the Pegu touch[3], which they call flowered silver, and if it flowers, it passes current.

Their way to make flowered silver is, when the silver and copper are mixed and melted together, and while the metal is liquid, they put it into a shallow mould, of what

---

[1] The turned-up part of the brim.
[2] The Cormandel coast of Southeast India, with Madras as its centre.
[3] Test.

figure or magnitude they please, and before the liquidity is gone, they blow on it through a small wooden pipe, which makes the face, or part blown upon, appear with the figures of flowers or stars, but I never saw any European or other foreigner at Pegu have the art to make those figures appear, and if there is too great a mixture of alloy, no figures will appear.

The king generally adds 10 per cent on all silver that comes into his treasury, besides what was put on at first, and though it be not flowered, it must go off in all his payments, but from anybody else it may be refused if it is not flowered.

His government is arbitrary. All his commands are laws, but the reins of government are kept steady and gently in the king's own hand. He severely punishes his governors of provinces or towns if oppressions or other illegal practices are proven upon them; and to know how affairs pass in the state, every province or city has a mandarin or deputy residing at court, which is generally in the city of Ava[1], the present metropolis.

Every morning these mandarins are obliged to attend at court, and after His Majesty has dressed and breakfasted, which is generally on a dish of rice boiled in fair water, and his sauce is some shrimps dried and powdered, and some salt and cod-pepper[2] mixed with those two ingredients, and that mixture makes a very pungent sauce, which they call *prock*[3], and is in great esteem and use among the Peguans.

When his breakfast is over, he retires into a room so contrived that he can see all the attendants, but none can

---

[1] Ava was the capital of Burma from 1364-1783 apart from two brief periods, 1628-35 and 1752-65.

[2] Pepper obtained from the pods.

[3] A Mon term; the fermented shrimp paste is also mentioned in Chapter Twelve, p.184 note 2.

see him, and a page stands without to call whom the king would have give account of the current news of his province or city, which is performed with profound reverence toward the room where the king stays, and with a distinct audible voice; and if any particular matters of consequence is forgot [*sic*] or omitted, and the king comes to hear of it by another hand, severe punishments follow, and so he passes his morning in hearing the necessary cases of his own affairs as well as those of his subjects.

If he is informed of treason, murder, or suchlike heinous crimes, he orders the matter to be judicially tried before judges of his own choosing, for that time and affair, and on conviction he signs the death warrant, wherein he orders that the wretch convicted shall tread no more on his ground, and execution presently follows, either by beheading, or ordering them [*sic*] to be sport for his elephants, which is the cruellest death. Sometimes he banishes them [*sic*] for a certain time to the woods, and if they are not devoured by tigers, or killed by wild elephants, they may return when their term is expired, and pass the remainder of their days in serving a tame elephant; and for smaller crimes they are only condemned to clean his elephants' stables for life.

His subjects, if they may be so called, treat him with fulsome adulation. When they speak or write to him they call him their god (or in their language *kiack*[1]) and in his letters to foreign princes he assumes the title of King of Kings, to whom all other kings ought to be subject, as being near kinsman and friend to all the gods in heaven and on earth, and by their friendship to him all animals are fed and preserved, and the seasons of the year are regularly kept: the sun is his brother, and the moon and stars are his near

---

[1]   '*Kyak*' meaning 'holy' (Mon).

relations, lord over the floods and ebbing of the sea; and after all his lofty epithets and hyperboles, he descends to be king of the white elephant, and of the twenty-four white sombreros[1] or umbrellas. These two last he may indeed claim with some show of justice, for I have seen elephants of a light yellow colour both in Pegu and Siam, but who ought to be called their lord is a question not yet decided; and as king of the twenty-four white sombreros, I believe few kings will much care to dispute that glorious title with him, for those sombreros are only common China umbrellas, covered over with thin Cormandel betelas, and their canes lacquered and gilded, and because his own subjects dare not use any such umbrellas, he wisely lays his imperial commands on all other kings to forebear wearing of them when they go abroad.

After His Majesty has dined, there is a trumpet blown, to signify to all his slaves, as he terms other kings, that they may go to dinner, because their lord has already dined. And when any foreign ships arrive at Syriam, the number of people on board, with their age and sex, are sent to him, to let him know that so many of his slaves are arrived to partake of the glory and happiness of his reign and favour, and the highest title his own subjects assume is the king's first slave.

The king's palace at Ava is very large, built of stone, and has four gates for its conveniencies. Ambassadors enter at the east gate, which is called the Golden Gate, because all ambassadors make their way to him by presents. The south gate is called the Gate of Justice, where all people that bring petitions, accusations, or complaints enter. The west is the Gate of Grace, where all that have received favours, or have

---

[1] Actually Hamilton writes 'somereroes', meaning parasols in the form of umbrellas.

been acquitted of crimes, pass out in state, and all condemned persons carried out in fetters; and the north gate fronting the river is the Gate of State where His Majesty passes through, when he thinks fit to bless his people with his presence, and all his provisions and water are carried in at that gate.

When pots of water, or baskets of fruits are carried through the streets for the king's use, an officer attends them, and all the people that fortune to be near must fall on their knees, and let it pass by, as a good Catholic does when he sees the host.

When an ambassador is admitted to audience in the palace, he is attended with a large troop of guards, with trumpets sounding, and heralds proclaiming the honour the ambassador is about to receive, in going to see the glory of the earth, His Majesty's own sweet face, and between the gate and the head of the stairs that lead to the chamber of audience, the ambassador is attended with the master of the ceremonies, who instructs him to kneel three times in his way thither, and continue so with his hands over his head, till a proclamation is read before he dare rise. Some of his elephants are instructed to fall on their belly when the king passes by them.

This relation I had from one Mr Roger Allanson[1], who had been twice ambassador from the governor of Fort St George[2], or his agents at Syriam, to the court of Ava; and though the palace is very large, yet the buildings are but mean, and the city though great and populous is only built of bamboo canes, thatched with straw or reeds, and the floors of teak plank, or split bamboos, because if treason or other capital crimes be detected, the criminals may have no

---

[1] He was known to have been an envoy in 1709.
[2] Madras.

place of shelter, for if they do not appear on the first summons, fire will fetch them out of their combustible habitations.

His sword officers have no salary, nor his soldiers for their support, but there is a province or a city given to some minion, who is to give sustenance to such a number of soldiers, and find [sic] the palace at Ava with such a quota of provisions as the provider thinks fit to appoint.

When there is a war, and parties are sent on expeditions, then the king allows them pay, clothes, arms, and provides magazines of provisions for them; but as soon as the war is at an end, then the clothes and arms are returned, by which means discipline is little known among them, and a man of a tolerable stock of courage may pass there for an hero.

The quality of an officer is known by his tobacco pipe having an earthen or metallic head, with a socket to let in a jointed reed, that on its upper end has a mouthpiece of gold, jointed as the reed or cane is, and by the number of joints in the golden mouthpiece the quality of the officer is known, and respect paid him accordingly.

All cities and towns under this king's dominions are like aristocratical commonwealths. The prince or governor seldom sits in council, but appoints his deputy, and twelve counsellors or judges, and they sit once in ten days at least, but oftener when business calls them. They convene in a large hall, mounted about three foot high, and double benches round the floor for people to sit or kneel on, and to hear the free debates of council. The hall, being built on pillars of wood, is open on all sides, and the judges set in the middle on mats, and sitting in a ring there is no place of precedence; there are no advocates to plead at the bar, but everyone has the privilege to plead his own cause, or send it in writing to be read publicly, and it is determined judicially within the term of three sittings of council, but if anyone questions his own eloquence, or knowledge of the laws of equity, he may empower a friend to plead for him, but there are no fees but what the town contributes for the maintenance of that court, which in their language is called the *rounday*[1], and those contributions are very small. There are clerks set at the backs of the judges ready to write down whatever the complainant and defendant has to say, and the case is determined by the prince and that council very equitably; for if the least partiality is found awarded to either party, and the king is made acquainted with it by the deputies at court, the whole sentence is revoked, and the whole board are corrected for it. So that very few have occasion to appeal to court, which they may do if they are aggrieved, and if an appeal is made upon ill grounds, the appellant is chastised, which just rigour hinders many tedious suits that arise where there are no penalties annexed to such faults.

The judges have a particular garb of their own. Their hair, being permitted to grow long, is tied on the top of their heads with cotton ribbon wrapped about it, and it stands upright in the form of a sharp pyramid. Their coat is of a thin betela, so that their skin is easily seen through it. About their loins they have a large *longhi*[2] or scarf, as all other Peguans have, that reaches to their ankles, and against the navel a round bundle made of their *longhi* as big as a child's head, but stockings and shoes are not used in Pegu.

The Burmese wear the same habit, and imprint several devices in their skins, pricked with a bodkin, and powder of charcoal rubbed over the little wounds, while the blood continues wet in them, and the black marks remain ever

[1]   In Burmese, *yondaw*.
[2]   Sarong.

after[1]. The Peguans dare not paint their skins, so that the natives of each nation are easily known by the distinguishing mark of painting or plainness. There are few of their men fat, but plump, well-shaped, of an olive colour, and well-featured.

The women are much whiter than the men, and have generally pretty plump faces, but of small stature, yet very well shaped, their hands and feet small, and their arms and legs well-proportioned. Their head-dress is their own black hair tied up behind, and when they go abroad, they wear a shawl folded up, or a piece of white cotton cloth lying loose on the top of their heads. Their bodily garb is a frock of cotton cloth or silk made meet for their bodies, and the arms of their frock stretched close on the arm, the lower part of the frock reaching half-thigh down. Under the frock they have a scarf or *longhi* doubled fourfold, made fast about their middle, which reaches almost to the ankle, so contrived that at every step they make as they walk, it opens before, and shows the right leg and part of the thigh[2].

This fashion of petticoats, they say, is very ancient, and was first contrived by a certain queen of that country, who was grieved to see the men so much addicted to sodomy[3] that they neglected the pretty ladies. She thought that by the sight of a pretty leg and plump thigh, the men might be

[1]   Hamilton is here describing the process of tattooing, without using the word, which did not enter English until later in the eighteenth century, from Polynesian.

[2]   Frank Vincent was to comment on this in *The Land of the White Elephant* (1874) pp.14-15. The men were held to be disfigured by tattoos and the woman thus more attractive in order that husbands did not give "themselves up to abominable vices".

[3]   This seems to be an old travellers' tale with little foundation; see Michael Smithies, 'Body ornamentation and penile implants in Siam and Pegu', *Journal of the Siam Society*, Vol. 82, in press.

allured from that abominable custom, and place their affections on proper objects, and according to the ingenious queen's conjecture, that dress of the *longhi* had its desired end, and now the name of sodomy is hardly known in that country.

The women are very courteous and kind to strangers, and are very fond of marrying with Europeans, and most part of the strangers who trade thither marry a wife for the term they stay. The ceremony is (after the parties are agreed) for the bride's parents or nearest friends or relations to make a feast, and invite her friends and the bridegroom's, and at the end of the feast, the parent or bridesman asketh them both, before the company, if they are content to cohabit together as man and wife, and both declaring their consent, they are declared by the parent or friend to be lawfully married; and if the bridegroom has an house, he carries her thither, but if not, they have a bed provided in the house where they are married, and are left to their own discretion how to pass away the night.

They prove obedient and obliging wives, and take the management of affairs within doors wholly in their own hands. She goes to market for food, and acts the cook in dressing his victuals, takes care of his clothes, in washing and mending them; if their husbands have any goods to sell, they set up a shop and sell them by retail, to a much better account than they could be sold for by wholesale, and some of them carry a cargo of goods to the inland towns, and barter for goods proper for the foreign markets that their husbands are bound to, and generally bring fair accounts of their negotiations. If she proves false to her husband's bed, and on fair proof convicted, her husband may carry her to the *rounday*, and have her hair cut, and sold for a slave, and he may have the money; but if the husband goes astray, she'll be apt to give him a gentle dose, to send him into the other world a sacrifice to her resentment.

If she proves prolific, the children cannot be carried out of the kingdom without the king's permission, but that may be purchased for £40 or £50 sterling; and if an irreconcilable quarrel happen where there are children, the father is obliged to take care of the boys, and the mother of the girls. If a husband is content to continue the marriage whilst he goes to foreign countries about his affairs, he must leave some fund to pay her about 6 shillings 8 pence per month, otherwise at the year's end she may marry again, but if that sum is paid her on his account, she is obliged to stay the term of three years; and she is never the worse, but rather the better looked on, that she has been married to several European husbands.

Monk passing through the town ('Talapoin allant par la ville') from
Guy Tachard, Voyage de Siam des Pères Jésuites... *(1686).*

CHAPTER TWO
[XXXVII]

THE CLERGY AND CUSTOMS
OF PEGU

G ives an account of the Pegu clergy, their charity, etc.,
their temples, and the reason why they are so
numerous, and their trials by ordeal, the fertility of the
country, and the ceremony in burning the corpse of an
high priest

The Pegu clergy are the best observers of the rules of
morality and charity that I have met with in my travels, and
the people are pious and hospitable. There are vast
numbers of temples built in this country, but most of wood,
because that material is plentifullest and cheapest, and
takes varnish and gilding best, being gaudily painted both
within and without. Everyone has free liberty to build a
baw[1] or temple, and when it is finished, purchases or
bestows a few acres of ground to maintain a certain number
of priests and novices, who manure and cultivate the
ground for their own sustenance, and in the garden the
priests and novices have a convent[2] built for their
conveniency of lodgings and study; and those are their
settled benefices, for they are no charge to the laity, but by

[1] The origin of the word is obscure.
[2] Monastery.

their industrious labour in managing their garden, they have enough for themselves, and something to spare to the poor indigent of the laity. But if their garden is too small or sterile for the subsistence of their family, then they send some novices abroad with a large orange-coloured mantle about their bodies, with a basket hanging on their left arm, a little drum in the left hand, and a little stick in the right, and when they come to the people's doors they beat three strokes with the stick on the drum, and if none come to answer, they beat again, and so on to the third time, and then if none answer, they proceed to the next house without speaking a word. But they are seldom sent away without an alms of rice, pulse, fruits, or roots, which is their only food, and what they receive more than they have present occasion for, they distribute to the poor, for they never take care for tomorrow; living all their days in celebacy, they have none of the anxiety of thinking about provision for a widow and children. Their innocent exemplary lives procure them many freewill offerings from the well-disposed laity, and what is saved after providing their convents of eatables and clothing, returns to the maintenance of the distressed laity, who, through age, sickness, or other accidents cannot maintain themselves by labour, but none who are able to work partake of their charity.

They preach or lecture frequently, and have a numerous auditory. Their religion is paganism[1] and their system of divinity polytheism. They have images in all their temples or *baws*, of inferior gods, such as Somma Cuddom [Samana Gautama], Samsay[2], and Prawpout[3], but they cannot form

[1]   It was of course Buddhism, but Hamilton was not able to recognize this.
[2]   See Chapter One, p.11 note 4.
[3]   *Phra Putta* [*Chao*], Lord Buddha.

an idea of the image of the great god, whose adoration is left to their tallapoies[1] or priests.

Those tallapoies or priests teach that charity is the most sublime virtue, and therefore ought to be extensive enough to reach not only to human species, but even to animals, wherefore they neither kill nor eat any, and they are so benevolent to mankind that they cherish all alike without distinction for the sake of religion. They hold all religions to be good that teach men to be good, and that the deities are pleased with variety of worship, but with none that is hurtful to men, because cruelty must be disagreeable to the nature of a deity: so being all agreed in that fundamental, they have but few polemics, and no persecutions, for they say that our minds are free agents, and ought neither to be forced nor fettered.

The images in their temples are placed in domes[2] in a sitting posture, with their legs across, their toes all alike long[3], their arms and hands very small in proportion to their bodies, their faces longer than human, and their ears large, and the lappets[4] very thick. The congregation bows to them when they come in and go out, and that is all the oblation they receive.

They never repair an old *baw*, nor is there any occasion for that piety or expense; for in every September there is an old custom for gentlemen of fortune to make sky rockets[5], and set them aflying in the air, and if any fly any great height, that is a certain sign that the owner is in favour with

---

[1] The more usual form is Talapoins, from Mon: *talapoe* meaning 'our lord', and was the standard word used by the French in the seventeenth century when talking of Siamese monks.

[2] Here, alcoves on altars.

[3] Hamilton correctly observes one of the signs of the Buddha.

[4] Lobes.

[5] This is still the custom in northeast Thailand, though the rockets are often associated with invocations for rain.

the gods, but if it comes to the ground, and spends its fire without rising, the owner is much dejected, and believes that the gods are angry with him, but the happy man, whose rocket makes him in the gods' favour, never fails of building a new *baw*, and dedicates it to the god he adores, and some priests, whose temples are gone to decay, bring their images to adorn it, who have the benefice for their pains.

I have seen some of those rockets so large that one of them could contain above five hundredweight of powder dust and coal, which is their common composition. The carcass is the trunk of a great tree made hollow, leaving about two inches of solid wood without[1] the cylinder, to strengthen it. The hollow they fill with the composition well rammed in, and after that is done, they make thongs of green buffaloes' hides, and hale tight[2] round the carcass to keep it from splitting, and those thongs are put from one end to the other, in the place of hoops; and when they grow dry, they are as close on the carcass as so many hoops. Then they secure the ends, that the composition may come gradually out when fired. The carcass they place on a branch of a large high tree, which grows plentifully in their fields, and fix it in the position they would have it mount in when fired, and then they take a large bamboo for a tail to balance it. Some I have seen above 120 foot long. When the tail is made fast according to art, then the day of solemnity is proclaimed, and great numbers of people of all ranks, degrees and ages assemble to see the rocket fly. When all are convened, the lashings that fastened it to the tree are cut, except so many as can support it from falling, and there are men with hatchets ready to cut them when the fire is

---

[1]   In the sense of 'outside'.
[2]   Draw forcibly.

put to it, which is done by the owner, and then the rocket takes flight, and some fly a prodigious height, others come to the ground, and fly five or six hundred paces in an irregular motion, wounding or scorching all that come in its way. The consequences of the high flier and the low I have described at length above.

A little while after the rockets' flying they have another feast, called the *collock*[1] and some women are chosen out of the people assembled to dance a dance to the gods of the earth. Hermaphrodites, who are numerous in this country, are generally chosen if there are enough present to make a set for the dance. I saw nine dance like mad folks for above half an hour, and then some of them fell in fits, foaming at the mouth for the space of half an hour; and, when their senses are restored, they pretend to foretell plenty or scarcity of corn for that year, if the year will prove sickly or salutary to the people, and several other things of moment, and all by that half-hour's conversation that the furious dancer had with the gods while she was in a trance.

They have various sorts of music, but the pipe and tabor are esteemed the best, though their stringed intruments pleased my ears best. They have one sort in [the] shape of a galley, with about twenty bells of several sizes and sounds, placed fast on the upper part, as it lies along. The instrument is about 3 foot long, and 8 or 10 inches broad, and 6 inches deep.[2] They beat those bells with a stick made of heavy wood, and they make no bad music.

There are two large temples near Syriam, so like one another in structure that they seem to be built by one model. One stands about six miles to the southward, called

[1] *Kedok,* or spirit dances. See Michael Smithies, 'Village Mons of Bangkok', *Journal of the Siam Society* 60/1 1972, p.328.

[2] This appears to be the Mon gong instrument, similar in sound if not in shape to the Javanese *bonang.*

Kiakiack[1], or the God of Gods temple. In it is an image of twenty yards long, lying in a sleeping posture[2], and, by their tradition, has lain in that posture 6,000 years. His doors and windows are always open, and everyone has the liberty to see him; and, when he awakes, this world is to be annihilated. The temple stands on an high champain ground[3], and may easily be seen, in a clear day, eight leagues off. The other stands in a low plain, north of Syriam, about the same distance, called Dagun[4]. His doors and windows are always shut, and none enters his temple but his priests, and they will not tell what shape he is of, only he is not of human shape. As soon as Kiakiack dissolves the being and frame of the world, Dagon or Dagun will gather up the fragments, and make a new one. There are yearly fairs held near those temples, and the free-will offerings arising at those fairs are for the use of the temples.

For finding out secret murder, theft or perjury, the trial of ordeal is much in custom in Pegu. One way is to make the accuser and the accused take some raw rice in their mouths, and chew, and swallow it, but he that is guilty of the crime alleged, or of false accusation, cannot swallow his morsel, but the innocent chews and swallows his easily.

Another way they have by driving a stake of wood into a river, and making the accuser and accused take hold of the stake, and keep their heads and bodies under water, and he who stays longest under water is the person to be credited, and whosoever is convicted by this trial, either for the crime alleged, or for malicious slander by accusation, must lie on his back three days and nights, with his neck in

[1]   South of Syriam.
[2]   A sleeping Buddha, at the moment of ascending to Nirvana.
[3]   Open country.
[4]   Shwe Dagon, Rangoon (now Yangon).

a pair of stocks, without meat or drink, and [is] fined to boot. They have also the custom of dipping the naked hand in boiling oil, or liquid lead, to clear them from atrocious crimes if accused, and if the accuser scalds himself in the trial, he must undergo the punishment due to the crime, which makes people very cautious how they calumniate one another. And, if anyone asperse a woman with the name of whore, and cannot prove the aspersion to be true, they are fined severely.

The country is fruitful and healthful, and the air so good that when strangers come hither in a bad state of health, they seldom fail of a speedy recovery; but the smallpox is dreaded as pestiferous, and in the province of Syriam[1] that distemper is most dangerous and most infectious, so that if anyone is seized by that disease, all the neighbourhood removes to two or three miles distance, and builds new houses, which are easily done with bamboos and reeds, which they have in great plenty. They leave with the diseased person a jar of water, a basket of raw rice, and some earthen pots to boil it in, then they bid him farewell for twenty-one days. If the patient has strength enough to rise and boil rice, he may then recover; if not, he must even die alone. And it is observable that, while a person has that distemper, the tiger, for all his voraciousness, will not touch him. If the patient dies within the term of twenty-one days, then the smell certifies them on their approaching the house, and if he live they carry him to their new built city, and make him a free burgess[2].

I saw the ceremony of an high priest's funeral, and was not a little pleased with the solemnity. After the corpse had been kept three or four months by spirits or gums from putrefaction, there was a great mast fixed in the ground so

---

[1]   The text has 'Kirian', probably a misprint.
[2]   A member of the borough, of the community.

fast that it could be moved no way from its perpendicular position. Then, about fifty or sixty yards on each side of that mast, four smaller masts were placed, and fixed perpendicularly in the ground. Around the great mast, in the middle, were erected three scaffolds above one another, the lowermost bigger than the second, and the third smaller than that, so that it looked like a pyramid four storeys high. The scaffolds were railed in on each side, except an open place of three or four foot wide on each side. All the scaffolds and the ground below them were filled with combustibles. From the mast in the middle four ropes were carried to the other four masts, and hauled tight, and a fire-rocket on each rope was placed at the respective small masts. Then the corpse was carried to the upper story of the pyramid, and laid flat on the scaffold, and, after a great show of sorrow among the people there present, a trumpet was sounded, which was a signal to set fire to the rockets, which in an instant flew with a quick motion along the ropes, and set fire to the combustibles, and in a moment they were all in a flame, so that in an hour or two all was consumed.

This high priest was held in so great veneration that he was reckoned a saint among the people. He was in great esteem with the king, and when any nobleman fell into disgrace, he used his interest with the king to have him restored again to favour, unless they were guilty of atrocious crimes, and in that case he used his endeavours to have the rigour of the punishment extenuated.

All the Pegu clergy are mediators in making up cases of debate and contention that happen among neighbours. They never leave mediating till there be a reconciliation, and, in token of friendship, according to an ancient custom there, they eat *champock*[1] from one another's hand, and

---

[1] As with eating tea (*min*) in northern Thailand; Hamilton may have confused the magnolia tree (*champak*) with the *letpet* tea bush.

that seals the friendship. This *champock* is tea of a very unsavoury taste; it grows as other tea does on bushes, and is in use on such occasions all over Pegu.

And now, since I must leave Pegu, I must not omit giving the clergy their due praises in another particular practice of their charity. If a stranger has the misfortune to be shipwrecked on their coast, by the laws of the country the men are the king's slaves, but, by the mediation of the church, the governors overlook that law; and when the unfortunate strangers come to their *baws*, they find a great deal of hospitality, both in food and raiment, and have letters of recommendation from the priests of one convent to those of another on the road they design to travel, where they may expect vessels to transport them to Syriam; and if any be sick or maimed, the priests, who are the Peguans' chief physicians, keep them in their convent till they are cured, and then furnish them with letters, as is above observed, for they never enquire which way a stranger worships God, but if he is human, he is the object of their charity.

There are some Christians in Syriam of the Portuguese offspring, and some Armenians. The Portuguese have a church, but the scandalous lives of the priests and people make them contemptible to all people in general.

I have only to add to my observations of Pegu that, in former times, Martaban was one of the most flourishing towns for trade in the east, having the benefit of a noble river, which afforded a good harbour for ships of the greatest burden; but, after the Burmese conquered it, they sunk a number of vessels full of stones in the mouth of the river, so that now it is unnavigable, except for small vessels. They make earthenware[1] there still, and glaze them with

---

[1]   Martaban jars were widely circulated in Southeast Asia from before the fourteenth century.

lead ore[1]. I have seen some jars made there that could contain two hogsheads[2] of liquor. They have also still a small trade in fish. Their mullet dried is the best dry fish I ever tasted, either in India or Europe.

The islands off the coast of Pegu are the Cocos[3], uninhabited, but full of coconut trees. They lie about twenty leagues west-south-west from Cape Negrais: and the islands Preparis[4] lie thirty-six leagues south of the said cape. They are high islands, uninhabited, and so environed with rocks under water that there is danger in landing on them. They seem to be overgrown with woods, and that is all that I could observe of them. There is another small island called Commoda[5], that lies about ten leagues of the coast of Pegu, but is not inhabited.

---

[1] White lead ore, cerussite, is used as a pigment and a glaze on jars.
[2] A hogshead contained about 50 imperial gallons (some 227 litres) in a large cask.
[3] The Coco group lies just north of the Andamans.
[4] Half way between the Cocos and Negrais.
[5] Unidentified; the coast down to Mergui is dotted with islands. It might be Kalegauk or the Moscos Islands.

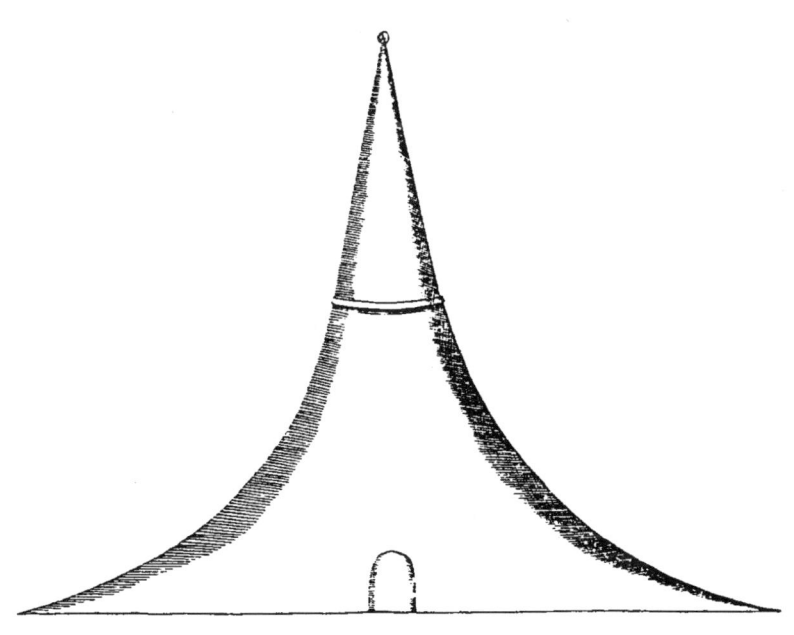

'A prospect of the Temple of Kiakeck or Dagunn' (the Shwe Dagon in Rangoon), apparently Hamilton's own sketch.

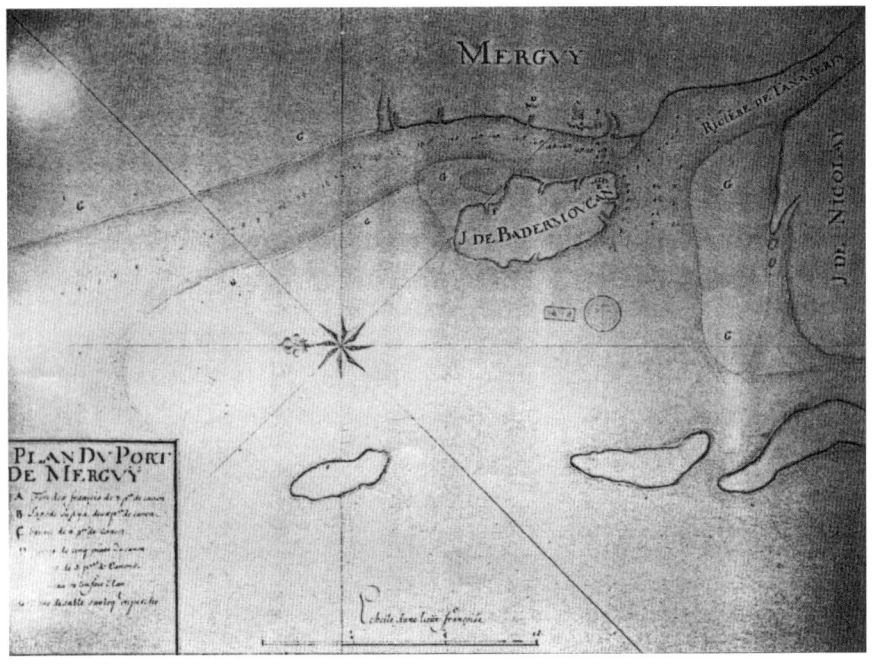

*Plan of the site of Mergui (end of the seventeenth century),
courtesy of Michel Jacq-Hergoualc'h.*

CHAPTER THREE
[XXXVIII]

SIAMESE MERGUI, TENASSERIM
AND PHUKET; KEDAH AND PERAK

Treats of Mergui and Tenasserim, and of the sea coast in the King of Siam's dominions, of the massacre there of the English in Anno 1687; also of Kedah and the other maritime countries and islands as far as Malacca

The next place on the continent, to the southward, is Mergui, a town belonging to the King of Siam, situated on the banks of the river of Tenasserim, lying within a great number of small uninhabited islands. The harbour is safe, and the country produces rice, timber for building, tin, elephants, elephants' teeth and agala-wood[1]. In former times a good number of English free merchants were settled at Mergui, and drove a good trade, living under a mild indulgent government; but the old East India Company, envying their happiness, by an arbitrary command, ordered them to leave their industry, and repair to Fort St George, to serve them, and threatened the King of Siam with a sea war if he did not deliver those English up

---

[1]   Also known as eaglewood, agalloch, calambac, agilawood, aloes wood. The fragrant resinous heartwood of the *aquilaria* was much traded in the seventeenth and early eighteenth centuries. Schouten notes it as one of the more important goods traded in Siam in 1636.

41

or force them out of his country, and in Anno 1687 sent one Captain Weldon[1] in a small ship called the *Curtana* to Mergui with that message[2]. He behaved himself very insolently to the government, and killed some Siamese without any just cause. One night when Weldon was ashore, the Siamese thinking to do themselves justice on him got a company together, designing to seize or kill the aggressor, but Weldon, having notice of their design, made his escape on board his ship, and the Siamese missing him though very narrowly, vented their rage and revenge on all the English they could find. The poor victims being only guarded by their innocence did not so much as arm themselves to withstand the fury of the enraged mob, so that seventy-six were massacred, and hardly twenty

[1]   Anthony Weltden, commander of the *Curtana*.
[2]   The background to the massacre of some 60 Englishmen at Mergui in July 1687 is complex, and not exactly as Hamilton would have it. The Levantine arriviste Phaulkon, effectively chief minister of Siam from 1683 to his downfall in 1688, had used private English traders, formerly like himself in the service of the EIC, and had commissioned private English ships for expeditions against the King of Golconda, with whom the Company was trying to be on good terms. Phaulkon also appointed Richard Burnaby as governor and Samuel White as shahbandar or habourmaster of Mergui, where they amassed fortunes. There was also the question of jewels ordered by Phaulkon from the Company, supposedly on behalf of King Narai, which had not been paid for. The Company demanded £65,000 from Narai and sent two ships to blockade Mergui. Burnaby and White were afraid of being charged with piracy in English courts, and entertained the commander Weltden and officers of the ships lavishly. The Siamese suspected the English intended to seize the port and on 14 July opened fire on the ships, killing every Englishman in sight. In August Narai declared war on the EIC and put Mergui in charge of a French governor, Beauregard, who came with handful of troops, to be succeeded in February 1688 by de Bruant.

escaped on board of the *Curtana*; so there was the tragical consequence of one man's insolence.

Before that fatal time, the English were so beloved and favoured at the court of Siam, that they had places of trust conferred upon them, both in the civil and military branches of the government[1]. Mr Samuel White was made shahbandar or custom-master at Mergui and Tenasserim, and Captain Williams[2] was admiral of the king's navy; but the troublesome Company, and a great revolution that happened in the state of Siam[3], made some repair to Fort St George, others to Bengal, and some to Aceh[4].

The islands opposite to the coast of Tenassarim are the Andemans[5]. They lie about eighty leagues off, and are surrounded with many dangerous banks and rocks; they are all inhabited with cannibals, who are so fearless that they will swim off to a boat if she approach near the shore, and attack her with their wooden weapons, notwithstanding the superiority of numbers in the boat, and the advantage of missive and defensive arms of iron, steel and fire.

I knew one Ferguson[6], who commanded a ship from Fort St George bound from Malacca to Bengal, in company with another ship, going too near one of the Andeman Islands, was driven by the force of a strong current on some

---

1   They were favoured by Phaulkon, though not necessarily beloved.
2   For Samuel White, see p. 42 note 2. Captain Williams, according to Foster, was a former second mate on the *Mexico President*.
3   The following year, 1688. A rather inaccurate account of the Siamese coup d'état appears later in Chapter Twelve.
4   Hamilton spells it Atcheen; the description follows in Chapter Six.
5   The Andeman islanders, between the Nicobars and Burma, were long credited with being cannibals.
6   A John Ferguson is listed among the 'seafaring men not constant inhabitants of Madras' in 1700.

rocks, and the ship was lost. The other ship was driven through a channel between two of the same islands, and was not able to assist the shipwrecked men, but neither Ferguson nor any of his people were ever more heard of, which gave ground to conjecture that they were all devoured by those savage cannibals.

I saw one of the natives of those islands at Aceh in Anno 1694. He was then about forty years of age. The Andemaners had a yearly custom to come to the Nicobar Islands[1] with a great number of small praus, and kill or take prisoners as many of the poor Nicobareans as they could overcome. The Nicobareans again joined their forces, and gave the cannibals battle when they met with them, and one time defeated them, and gave no quarter to the Andemaners. This man above-mentioned, when a boy of ten or twelve years of age, accompanied his father in the wars, and was taken prisoner, and his youth recommending him to mercy, they saved his life and made him a slave. After he had continued so three or four years, he was carried to Aceh to be sold for cloth, knives and tobacco which are the commodities most wanting on the Nicobars. The Achinese being Muhammadans, this boy's patron bred him up in that religion, and some years after, his master dying, gave him his freedom; he having a great desire to see his native country took a prau, and the months of December, January and February being fair weather and the sea smooth, he ventured to the sea in order to go to his own country, from the islands of Gomus and Pulau Wey[2]

---

[1] These lie between the Andemans and north Sumatra, and are described below.

[2] Gomus, also known as Kelapa, and Wey are both mentioned again at the end of Chapter Six. Hamilton spells the Malay for island, *pulau,* 'pullo'. Wey is sometimes spelt Wai, We or Weh.

which lie near Aceh. Here the southernmost of the Nicobars may be seen, and so one island may be seen from another, from the southernmost of those to Chitty Andeman[1], which is the southermost of the Andemans, which are distant from Aceh about an hundred leagues. Arriving among his relations he was made welcome, with great demonstrations of joy to see him alive, whom they expected to have been long dead.

Having retained his native language, he gave them an account of his adventures; and, as the Andemaners have no notions of a deity, he acquainted them with the knowledge he had of a god, and would have persuaded his country-men to learn of him the way to adore God, and to obey His laws, but he could make no converts. When he had stayed a month or two, he took leave to be gone again, which they permitted on condition that he would return. He brought along with him four or five hundredweight of quicksilver[2] and he said that some of the Andeman Islands abound in that commodity. He had made several trips thither before I saw him, and always brought some quicksilver along with him. Some Muhammadan fakirs[3] would fain have accompanied him in his voyages, but he would never suffer them, because he said he could not engage for their safety among his countrymen. When I saw him, he was in company with a sayyid[4], whom I carried a passenger to Surat[5], and from him I had this account of his adventures.

---

[1]   Little Andeman.
[2]   Mercury, which is not normally a commodity exported from the Andemans.
[3]   A Muslim mendicant or ascetic.
[4]   A descendant of the Prophet.
[5]   A major trading port of the period in northwest India, north of Bombay, with English, French and Dutch 'factories'.

The next place of any commerce on this coast is the island of Junk Ceylon[1]. It lies in the dominions of the King of Siam. Between Mergui and Junk Ceylon there are several good harbours for shipping, but the sea coast is very thin of inhabitants, because there are great numbers of freebooters, called saleiters[2], who inhabit islands along the sea coast, and they both rob and take people for slaves, and transport them for Aceh and there make sale of them, and Junk Ceylon often feels the weight of their depredations.

The north end of Junk Ceylon lies within a mile of the continent[3], but the south end is above three leagues from it. Between the island and the continent is a good harbour for shipping in the southwest monsoons, and on the west side of the island Puton Bay[4] is a safe harbour in the northeast winds. The islands afford good masts for shipping, and abundance of tin, but few people to dig for it, by reason of the aforementioned outlaws, and the governors being generally Chinese, who buy their places at the court of Siam[5], and to reimburse themselves oppress the people, insomuch that riches would be but a plague to them, and their poverty makes them live an easy indolent life.

Yet the villages on the continent drive a small trade with shipping that come[s] from the Cormandel Coast and Bengal, but both the buyer and seller trade by retail, so that

1 The old name for Phuket, derived from the Malay *ujong silang*, Cape Challang. Hamilton spells it 'Jonkceyloan'.
2 They were simply pirates, or piratical adventurers. The etymology of *saleiters* is found in the Malay *selat*, meaning strait; they lay in wait in the straits.
3 The distance is much less than one mile, and is now spanned by a bridge.
4 This is the first known reference to Patong Bay.
5 Chinese tax farmers in Phuket, Ranong and Songkhla continued to operate well into the nineteenth century.

a ship's cargo is a long time in selling, and the product of the country is as long in purchasing.

The islands off this part of the coast are the Nicobars, and are about ninety leagues distant from the continent. The northmost cluster is low, and are called the Carnicubars, and by their vicinity to the Andemans are but thinly inhabited. The middle cluster is fine champain ground, and all but one well inhabited. They are called the Somerera Islands, because on the south end of the largest island is an hill that resembles the top of an umbrella or somerera. About six leagues to the southward of Somerera Island lies Tallang-jang, the uninhabited island where one Captain Owen lost his ship in Anno 1708, but the men were all saved, and finding no inhabitants they made fires in the night, and next day there came five or six canoes from Ning and Goury, two fine islands that lie about four leagues to the westward of the desert island, and very courteously carried the shipwrecked men to their islands of Ning and Goury, with what little things they had saved of their apparel and other necessaries[1].

The captain had saved a broken knife about four inches long in the blade, and he having laid it carelessly by, one of the natives made bold to take it, but did not offer to hide it. The captain, seeing his knife in the poor native's hand, took it from him, and bestowed some kicks and blows on him

---

[1]   Foster (1930) says: "What Hamilton calls 'the northernmost cluster' is practically one island, Car Nicobar. The 'middle cluster' consists of Teressa, Camorta, Katchall, Nancowry, and some smaller islands. The group has lost the name of 'Somerera Islands', but the passage to the south is still called Sombreiro Channel. 'Tallang-jang' is presumably the coral bank to the south of Katchall. 'Ning' and 'Goury' seem to be not two but one island, viz. Nancowry; but that is N.E. of the coral bank. From the account our author gives of the Nicobars, it is clear that he had actually visited them."

for his ill manners, which was very ill-taken, for all in general showed they were dissatisfied with the action; and the shipwrecked men could observe contentions arising between those who were their benefactors in bringing them to their island, and others who were not concerned in it. However, next day as the captain was sitting under a tree at dinner, there came about a dozen of natives towards him, and saluted him on every side with a shower of darts made of heavy hard wood, with their points hardened in the fire, and so he expired in a moment. How far they had a mind to pursue their resentment, I know not, but their benefactors kept guard about their house till next day, and then presented them with two canoes, and fitted them with outleagers[1] to keep them from overturning, and put some water in pots, some coconuts and dried fish, and pointed to them to be immediately gone, which they did. Being sixteen in company, they divided equally, and steered their course for Junk Ceylon, but in the way one of the boats lost her outleager, and drowned all her crew. The rest arrived safe, and I carried them afterwards to Matchulipatam[2].

Ning and Goury are two fine smooth islands, well inhabited, and plentifully furnished with several sorts of good fish, hogs and poultry, but they have no horses, cows, sheep, nor goats, nor wild beasts of any sort but monkeys. They have no rice nor pulse, so that the kernel of coconuts, yams, and potatoes serves them for bread.

Along the north end of the eastmost of the two islands are good soundings from ten to eight fathoms sand, about two miles off the shore. The people come thronging on board in their canoes, and bring hogs, fowl, cocks, fish

---

[1]   Outriggers.
[2]   Also known as Masulipatam and Masulipatnam, and now called Bandar, a major trading port on the east coast of India.

48

fresh, salted and dried, yams the best I ever tasted, potatoes, parrots and monkeys, to barter for old hatchets, swordblades, and thick pieces of iron hoops, to make defensive weapons against their common disturbers and implacable enemies the Andemaners; and tobacco they are very greedy of. For a leaf of tobacco, if pretty large, they will give a cock, for three foot of an iron hoop, a large hog, and for one foot in length a pig. They all speak a little broken Portuguese, but what religious worship they use I could not learn.

The island Somerera lies about eight leagues to the northward of Ning and Goury, and is well-inhabited by the number of villages that show themselves as we sail along its shores. The people, like those of Ning and Goury, are very courteous, and bring the product of their island aboard of ships to exchange for the aforementioned commodities. Silver nor gold they neither have nor care for, so the root of all evil can never send out branches of misery, or bear fruit to poison their happiness. The men's clothing is a bit of string round their middle, and about a foot and an half of cloth six inches broad, tucked before and behind within that line. The women have a petticoat from the navel to the knee, and their hair close shaved, but the men have the hair left on the upper part of the head, and below the crown, but cut so short that it hardly comes to their ears.

The southward cluster of the Nicobars is mountainous, and the people partake of its unpolished nature, being more uncivil and surly than those to the northward. Their islands produce the same necessaries as the others do.

Kedah[1] is the next place of note on the continent to the southward, and is honoured with the title of a kingdom,

---

[1]   Hamilton has the spelling Quedah throughout. The present capital, Alor Star, is 10 km from the coast.

though both small and poor. The town which bears the same name stands on the banks of a small navigable river, deep, but narrow, about fifty miles from the sea, and the king resides in it, but shows no marks of grandeur, besides arbitrary governing.

Their religion is Muhammadan, much mixed with paganism[1]. The people are deceitful, covetous, and cruel. It was many years tributary to Siam, but in their long Pegu war, it threw off the yoke[2]. Its product is tin, pepper, elephants and elephants' teeth, canes, and damar, a gum that is used for making pitch and tar for the use of shipping. The king is poor, proud, and beggarly; he never fails of visiting stranger merchants at their coming to his port, and then, according to custom, he must have a present. When the stranger returns the visit, or has any business with him, he must make him a present, otherwise he thinks due respect is not paid to him, and in return of these presents His Majesty will honour the stranger with a seat near his sacred person, and will chew a little betel, and put it out of his royal mouth on a little gold saucer, and sends it by his page to the stranger, who must take it with all the signs of humility and satisfaction, and chew it after him, and it is very dangerous to refuse the royal morsel.

Some ages ago, Ligor was a kingdom of itself, and the kings of Kedah and Ligor[3] fell at variance. He of Kedah

[1]   As seen from Chapter Two, Hamilton equates Buddhism with paganism, so rather than referring to animistic practices, he may well intend Buddhism here.

[2]   Kedah was conquered by Aceh in 1619 but later Siam reasserted itself, though its overlordship of Kedah often meant little. Kedah continued to send the *bunga mas* or golden flowers of fealty to the Siamese capital though at the same time occasionally sought Burmese protection and later, by ceding Penang to the British, hoped for British support.

[3]   The sultan of Kedah and the governor of Nakhon Si Thammarat (see

invaded the territories of Ligor, and left his queen and his son, an hopeful youth about twenty years of age, to govern in his absence. The mother and son grew enamoured of each other, and she found herself with child by the reciprocal esteem they bore one another. She being justly afraid of the king's resentment on his return, laid the danger before her son that threatened them both, and advised the dutiful child to prevent their death by killing his father. Whereupon he wrote to the king for leave to give him a visit in the camp, which favour he obtained, and proceeded accordingly to the place where his father was with his army. At his arrival he was received by all with great demonstrations of joy, particularly by his father, who made him lodge in his own tent. The villain let his father fall asleep, and then stabbed him to the heart, and immediately left the army, and hast[en]ed to his loving mother to give her an account of his noble action. In the morning, the king being found dead and the son gone, the regicide was soon known; and because the queen should not continue long a widow, the obedient child married her himself, because none in the country had royal blood in their veins but himself, and she could not stoop to match below the dignity of a sovereign prince. Such libidinous marriages are very frequent in this country to this present time[1].

p.16 note 2). The hereditary governors of Ligor were long thought by outsiders to be kings in their own right, rather than vassals of Siam, and they were not disabused until the early nineteenth century.

[1]   The source of this story is again found in Mendes Pinto. Chapter 19: "At the time we arrived in Kedah, the king was in the midst of conducting elaborate funeral services for his father, whom he had stabbed to death in order to marry his mother who was pregnant with his child..."(*The Travels of Mendes Pinto*, ed. Rebecca Catz, 1989). It has to be added that the problems of finding a spouse of suitable

Perak[1] is the next country to Kedah. It is properly a part of the Kingdom of Johor, but the people are untractable and rebellious, and the government anarchical. Their religion is heterodox Muhammadanism. The country produces more tin than any in India, but the inhabitants are so treacherous, faithless, and bloody that no European nation can keep factories there with safety. The Dutch tried it once, and the first year had their factory cut off. They then settled on Pulau Dinding[2], an island at the mouth of the river Perak[3], but about the year 1690 that factory was also cut off, and I never heard that anybody else ever attempted to settle there since.

There are several other places along that coast of Malaya that produce great quantities of tin, but Selangor and Parsalore[4] are the most noted, though little frequented by Europeans, because they have too many of the Perak qualities to be trusted with honest men's lives and money. Their religion is also a sort of scoundrel Muhammadanism.

rank often led to what would now be considered incestuous relationships.

[1] Perak was rich in tin. The Dutch secured an agreement in 1650 to exploit it, but in 1651 the factory was attacked and nine officials killed.

[2] Pulau Pangkor. The Dutch rebuilt their fort in 1745; it is now appropriately called Kota Belanda.

[3] Pangkor is actually opposite the mouth of the Sungei Dinding; the Perak River is a little further south.

[4] Now the mouth of the Klang River, by Port Klang; Klang itself was at one stage the state capital of Selangor.

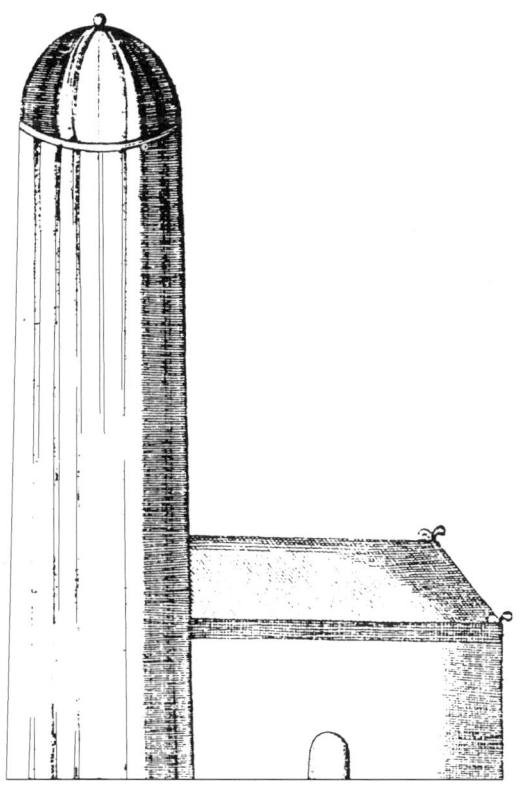

*'The Temple of Praprumb: The Steeple Gilded with Gold on the outside'
(possibly meant to be Wat Sri Sanphet, Ayutthaya),
apparently Hamilton's own sketch.*

View of Malacca in 1678, from Balthasar Bort, Report on Malacca....

MALACCA

G ives an account of Malacca, how the Portuguese got
footing there, and fortified it, and how the Dutch
supplanted the Portuguese, and made it a colony of theirs,
with some occurrences happening to the Scots Company's
affairs there, and other places in India

Malacca[1] is the next place in course along this coast of
Malaya. Before the Portuguese came to India[2] it had been
the place of residence of the kings of Johor, but they
denying the Portuguese commerce in their country,
associated themselves with the King of Aru[3] (a potent
prince in those times) on the island of Sumatra, who was

---

[1] Founded by Parameswara, probably of Palembang, in 1399 or 1400,
    it quickly became a great trading centre, and, after its sultans
    converted to Islam, a centre of the spread of Islam in Southeast Asia.
    The last sultan, Mahmud, fled to Pahang and then to Johor.
[2] The meaning here, as elsewhere in the text, is 'the East Indies'; the
    Portuguese attacked and conquered Malacca in 1511, the year after
    acquiring Goa. The Sultan of Malacca was at war at the time with the
    King of Aru.
[3] Aru was formely a powerful kingdom in northeast Sumatra but was
    vanquished by Aceh in the sixteenth century. The name survives in
    Marsden's map (1811) marking some islands in the straits between
    Asahan River and Selangor.

engaged in a war with the King of Johor, and with their joint forces obliged him to quit that place, and retire to Johor Lama which lies at the very point of that promontory, within one degree of the equator. There is a noble spacious river that accommodates Johor Lama[1].

As soon as the King of Johor was gone, the Portuguese began to fortify, and encompassed a little hill with a stone wall about a mile round, in which they built a city, and called it Malacca, and by the conveniency of its situation in a few years it became the greatest mart in India; however, the King of Johor was fain to make a peace with the Portuguese, allowing them their fort, and as much ground round it as their cannon could sling a shot, and so they became friends; but the King of Johor invaded the King of Aru's dominions, with a numerous fleet of galleys, and in a short time forced him to crave aid from the Portuguese, who never used to deceive their allies but when they trusted to them, and so the King of Aru lost his country.

Malacca, a place of small account, in a short time became famous all over India and Europe, lying almost in the centre of trade brought thither by shipping from the rich kingdoms of Japan, China, Formosa, Luconia[2], Tonkin, Cochin-China, Cambodia, and Siam, besides what Johor produced, and Sumatra, Java, Borneo, Makassar, Banda, Amboina, and Ternate Islands[3], that produce many valuable commodities.

As the Portuguese grew great and rich, they grew also insolent, and so continued abusing and affronting their

---

[1]   Old Johor, some 16 km up Johor River. Mahmud's son Alauddin settled at Johor Lama which was captured by the Portuguese in 1536 and by Aceh in 1564.

[2]   Luzon.

[3]   'Sumatra...Ternate' are all mentioned in detail further on in the text.

neighbours till about the year 1660[1], the Dutch had a war with Portugal, on account of some losses the Dutch sustained in Brazil.

The Dutch sent many ships and good forces to India, to be equal with the Portuguese, for their driving the Dutch out of Brazil; and how their arms flourished on the coasts of Malabar[2] and Ceylon I have observed already in my first volume, and so I begin again at Malacca.

The Dutch coming into the Straits of Malacca from Batavia[3] with a strong fleet and a land army on board of it, struck up an alliance with the King of Johor, offensive and defensive, as long as the sun and moon gave light to this world; for I saw the treaty, and heard it read, with those expressions in it: on which the King of Johor assisted the Dutch with 20,000 men, and laid siege to the fort by land, while the Dutch distressed it by sea; and yet for all that the fleet and army could do, they could not have taken it by force, but by reducing them by famine, which would have taken up a great deal of time, so what they could not effect by force, they did by fraud.

They heard that the Portuguese governor was a sordid avaricious fellow, and ill-beloved by the garrison, so the Dutch, by secret conveyances, tampered with him by letters, promising him mountains of gold if he would contribute towards their gaining the fort. At length the price was set of 80,000 pieces of eight to be the reward of his treachery, and to be safely transported to Batavia in their fleet, and be made a free denizen[4] there. So he sent secret orders to the Dutch to make an attack on the east side

---

[1]   Malacca was besieged by the Dutch in 1633; it fell, with help from the Sultan of Johor, in January 1641.

[2]   The southwest coast of India, between Goa and Cape Comorin.

[3]   Now Jakarta. Batavia is described rather cursorily in Chapter Nine.

[4]   A foreigner admitted to residence and given certain rights.

of the fort, and he would act his part, which was accordingly done[1].

He thereupon called a council, and told them he had a mind to circumvent the Dutch by letting them come close to the fort walls, and then to fire briskly on them from all quarters, and destroy them at once, so the Dutch made their approaches without molestation, and placed their ladders. The garrison sent message after message to acquaint the governor of the danger they were in, for want of orders to fire and sally out on the Dutch, as was agreed on in council, but he delayed so long till the Dutch got into the fort, and drove the guard from the east gate, which they soon opened to receive the rest of their army, who, as soon as they were entered, gave quarters to none that were in arms, and marching towards the governor's house, where he thought himself secure by the treaty, they forthwith dispatched him to save the fourscore thousand dollars.

The master gunner being posted on a large bastion, whose walls are washed by the sea at high water, with about 100 Portuguese along with him, would by no means yield till he had capitulated with the Dutch for fair quarter for himself and his company, which the Dutch would not adhere to, so that for two days he gallantly maintained his post. At last, by continual fatigue, and loss of his men, he was obliged to yield to fate and great superiority of numbers, and died like an hero with his sword in his hand; and there is a common report at Malacca still that the night after the aniversary day of his death his genius[2] is seen on that bastion. And I was informed by a Dutch governor at Malacca that on that night no sentinels are set there, for that several have found the effects of his fury, by being thrown

---

[1]   This story and its consequence appear to have no foundation in fact.
[2]   Ghost.

over the wall, and have been either killed or maimed by the fall.

The Portuguese, to show their zeal to religion while they were masters of Malacca, had no less than three churches and a chapel within the fort, and one without, but now there is but one church and a chapel within, and none without. That which the Dutch now use for their worship stands conspicuously on the top of the hill[1], and may be seen up or down the straits at a good distance, and a flagstaff is placed on the steeple, on which a flag is hoisted on the sight of any ship.

The fort is both large and strong, the sea washing the walls of one third part of it, and a deep, rapid but narrow river the west side of it, and a broad deep ditch [round] the rest of it. The governor's house is both beautiful and convenient, and there are several other good houses in the fort and in the town without the fort, but the road for shipping is at too great a distance to be defended by the fort, the shallowness of the sea obliging them to lie above a league off, which is a very great inconveniency. For in 1709, the French coming into the straits with a squadron of three or four sail, seeing a large ship in the road newly arrived from Japan stood into the road, and had certainly carried her out, if the wind had not failed them about [a] musket shot from her.

At Malacca the straits are not above four leagues broad; for though the opposite shore on Sumatra is very low, yet it may easily be seen in a clear day, which is the reason that the sea is always as smooth as a millpond, except when it is

---

[1] The church was dedicated by the Portuguese to Nossa Senhora da Annunciada, but after the Dutch seizure of Malacca in 1641 was reconsecrated as a Dutch Reformed Church and dedicated to St Paul. It was later abandoned by the Dutch in favour of the red brick Christ Church, built in 1753 close to the Stadthuys.

ruffled with squalls of wind, which seldom come without lightnings, thunder, and rain; and though they come with great violence, yet they are soon over, not often exceeding an hour.

The country produces nothing for a foreign market, but a little tin and elephants' teeth, but several excellent fruits and roots for the use of the inhabitants and strangers who call there for refreshments. The Malacca pineapple is accounted the best in the world, for in other parts, if they are eaten to a small excess, they are apt to give surfeits, but those of Malacca never offend the stomach. The mangosteen is a delicious fruit, almost in the shape of an apple; the skin is thick and red, [and] being dried it is a good astringent. The kernels (if I may so call them) are like cloves of garlic, of a very agreeable taste, but very cold. The rambutan is a fruit about the bigness of a walnut, with a tough skin, beset with capillaments[1]; within the skin is a very savoury pulp. The durian is another excellent fruit, but offensive to some people's noses, for it smells very like human excrements, but when once tasted, the smell vanishes. The skin is thick and yellow, and within is a pulp like thick cream in colour and consistence, but more delicious in taste. The pulp or meat is very hot and nourishing, and instead of surfeiting, they fortify the stomach, and are a great incentive to wantonness. They have coconuts in plenty, and some grow in marshes that are overflown with the sea in spring tides. Their liquor and kernel partake of the qualities of the ground they grow in, being exceeding salt. I never saw any coconuts grow in salt grounds but there, and some are so large that the shell will hold more than an English quart pot[2]. They have also

[1]   Hairs.
[2]   More than one litre.

plenty of lemons, oranges, limes, sugar canes, and mangoes[1]. They have a species of mango called by the Dutch a stinker[2], which is very offensive both to the smell and taste, and consequently of little use. There is little corn or pulse [that] grows in this country but what is nourished in gardens.

Sheep and bullocks are scarce and dear, but swines' flesh, poultry, and fish pretty plentiful, and reasonably cheap, considering it is a Dutch colony, whose excessive taxes make everything dear, and discourage the poor from improving, since poverty secures them from further oppression. Their corn comes all from Java, Siam, or Cambodia, but the freight makes it come out dear to what it is in other places whose native ground produces it.

I will pass by their court of justice, because it hardly deserves the name, since strangers are excluded from the common laws of humanity, wherein I am able to give many instances, but I voluntarily pass by particularities till another time.

There is a very high mountain[3] to the north-eastward of Malacca, that sends forth several rivers, of which that to Malacca is one, and all of them have small quantities of gold-dust found in their channels. The inland inhabitants called Minangkabau[4] are a barbarous savage people, whose greatest pleasure is in doing mischief to their neighbours,

---

[1] Every text of the period has a section on exotic fruits to be found in the region; Hamilton's is no exception.

[2] Either a fetid mango, or else a kind of durian.

[3] Mount Ophir, now Gunung Ledang.

[4] Hamilton, who spells them Monacoboes, confuses the Minangkabau, many of whom came from west-central Sumatra to settle in peninsular Malaya, with what are now known as the *orang asli* (the Negritos, the Senoi, and the proto-Malays), the original inhabitants of the peninsula, who were driven inland.

which is the greatest reason why the peasants about Malacca sow no grain but what is enclosed in gardens with thick-set prickly hedges or deep ditches; for when their grain is ripe in the open plains, the Minangkabau never fail of putting fire to it, in order to consume it. They are much whiter than their neighbouring Malays who inhabit the low grounds, and the kings of Johor, whose subjects they are, or at least ought to be, could never civilize them.

Their religion is a complex of Muhammadanism and paganism, and they have the character of great sorcerers, who by their spells can tame wild tigers, and make them carry them whither they order them on their backs. Once they had a mind to try their art on the town of Malacca, but were unsuccessful in their enterprise, according to common report there. For one of their chief wizards assured them that neither gun, sword, nor lance should have power to hurt them, if they should attempt the town, whose defence consists only in a slight gate, with a little round bastion, with five or six great guns mounted on it. So on the opinion of their doctor's art, a great number drew together, and being armed with lance and kris, their common weapons, marched without order or fear towards the gate. When they came near enough, the gunner of the bastion pointed some guns, and set fire to the priming, but that flashed, and the guns would not discharge, which discouraged the guard of the gate; but a Malay soldier, who understood some of the Minangkabau art, called for a piece of pork, with which he besmeared the mouths of the cannon, while the gunner renewed the priming, and fire being put to them, the cannon went off and did good execution, which so frightened the Minangkabaus that they betook themselves to flight, and never attempted to disturb the town since.

I saw strange cures performed by a Malay doctor at Malacca. One of them was on a gentleman of my acquaintance, who was second supercargo[1] of a Scots ship[2] called the *Speedwell,* which was lost near Malacca. After the ship was lost, the first supercargo[3] took an house near the town, by the seaside, to put their cargo and stores in that were saved, but eleven chests of treasure and some fine goods were lodged in one of the Dutch Company's warehouses in the fort, which had three locks on its door. The governor had one key, and each of the supercargoes one. A common strumpet[4] called Mistress Kennedy, who at that time was married to on Irish pirate of that name, and kept an ordinary[5] in Malacca, gave the first supercargo a philtre that made him dote on her almost to distraction. He was never easy out of her company while awake, and in his sleep he called her by name. When she had got him so far in the noose, she pretended she had great need of money, and would fain have borrowed a chest of £1,000 sterling of the Scots Company's money. The bewitched supercargo could deny her nothing she asked for, and promised that if he could bring his second to consent, she should have it, but that consent could be got on no terms, though the first proffered to be accountable to their masters for that sum. And he acquainting her with the impossiblity of getting that consent, she contrived a way to remove the second by poison, and, going to a female friend of hers who was well acquainted with the mystery of poisoning, procured a dose so small that she could drop it in his broth or drink without his perceiving it; and accordingly she took an opportunity

---

1   A person managing sales on a merchant ship; the second supercargo of the *Speedwell* (whose captain was John Campbell) was Walter Keir.
2   Belonging to the short-lived Scottish East India Company in 1701. Hamilton gives further details of the company and the ship below.
3   By name Robert Innes.
4   Prostitute.
5   A tavern.

to dine with them one day when they had broth at table, and in serving the broth about, she dropped it among his. The same night it began to operate by gripings and sweating, and he being bred a surgeon, took some medicines to correct the gripings, which in some measure the medicine did, but he lost his appetite, and his excrements came from him as black as ink. In the interim a ship came from Surat bound to China, wherein the chief supercargo was obliged to embark with the Company's stock, and left the second at Malacca to take care of what was left there. A few days after the Surat ship sailed, I arrived at Malacca, and found the second supercargo in a deplorable condition.

He, finding all medicines ineffectual, began to fear poison, and sent for the Dutch doctor of physic to consult him, who, on sight of his excrements, told him plainly that he was poisoned, and advised him to send for a noted Malay doctor, who lived at a place called Batantiga[1], about four miles to the northwest of Malacca, which he forthwith did. And when the doctor came, he felt his pulse, and immediately told [him] that he was poisoned, and that if he could not tell what poison he had taken, his cure was very desperate and uncertain. I advised my friend to let old Beelzebub (for he was a man or walking shadow of a dismal aspect, near an hundred years old) take him into his care. My friend took my advice, and complimented the doctor with five Japan kupangs[2], or fifty Dutch dollars. Old Aesculapius[3] laughed when he received the present, but

---

[1] Untraced near Malacca; a Batantiga existed in Sumatra.
[2] Japanese gold coins, also called 'copangs', with some circulation in the region, worth ten rix dollars each. The term 'kuping' was also current in China, and was a treasury scale for silver.
[3] The Roman god of medicine, identified with the Greek Asclepius, son of Apollo.

could not show one tooth, but promised his utmost endeavours to cure him. He asked my friend if he suspected anybody particularly who might owe him a grudge. He answered none but Mistress Kennedy, or some of her companions. The doctor called for a teacup, and some fresh limes, which were brought to him. He turned all out of the room but myself and his patient, and cut some limes, and squeezed their juice into the teacup till it was full. He then muttered some unintelligible words, keeping his right hand moving over the cup for the space of three or four minutes, and finding his conjuration was not satisfactory, he shaked his old head, and looked dejected. He then muttered some other words with an higher voice, keeping his hand in motion as before, and in two minutes the juice in the cup seemed to boil as if fire had been under it. Then he began to smile. I had the curiosity to put my finger into the juice, but it retained its ordinary coldness. He then told his patient that his cure was certain, on which he had a promise of five kupangs more when the cure was effected. He ordered the patient to send a servant to Mistress Kennedy's door, and watch between the hours of ten and twelve, and to observe well if there was any unusual noise in her house between those hours, and so took his leave with a contented countenance. At ten my friend sent a servant according to direction, and he and I sat discoursing about what we had observed in the doctor's actions towards effecting the cure. About eleven the spy came and told us that Mistress Kennedy had run stark mad, making an hideous noise, and said she had seen the devil in the little house in the garden, in a monstrous shape and terrible aspect. She soon after grew furiously mad, scratching and biting everybody she could come at, and so the family was forced to throw her on a bed, and tie her down to it.

In that fit she continued till about eight in the morning, that the old conjurer came to town, who, upon the advice given him, went directly to visit her. Upon sight of him she became calm and sensible. He ordered everybody out of the room, and asked her what poison she had given to his patient. She was very loath to tell, and proffered him 500 dollars to forsake his patient, and let the poison operate; but he honestly refused, and assured her that the same devil that she saw in the garden should be her continual companion all her days, and would often make her feel the effects of his power, if she did not instantly declare what the poison was, and from whom she had it. She seeing no other remedy, confessed where she had the poison, but could not tell what it was. The doctor sent for the old schoolmistress of wickedness, and when she came, he threatened to torment her also by his humble servant the devil if she did not forthwith declare what poison had been given, which she did, and he took away Mistress Kennedy's companion the devil, and the patient was well enough in eight or ten days to follow his affairs, but Mistress Kennedy looked ever after disturbed, as if continually frightened.

Another strange cure I saw him perform on an officer belonging to my ship. He was going to sleep about midnight, and lying down on his bed, was bit in the calf of the leg by a centipede, an insect with many feet and very venomous. The pain that the bite caused would allow him no rest. Next day he expected that the venom might have been exhausted, but in that he was mistaken, for it grew first red by inflamation, and then blue and numbed. I sent for the doctor aforesaid, who came on the first summons. I told him of the accident that had happened, and he said there was no danger. He saw the inflamed leg, and kept his hand moving over it, but did not touch it. He muttered some unintelligible words, and spat on the place affected, and in five minutes he could walk without pain, though before the cure he could not stand without something to support him.

And since I have been mentioning the Scots East India ship and her supercargoes, I will give a small account of the management of their affairs in India. They arrived at Batavia about the beginning of July 1701 but being taken up with the pleasures of the place, loitered away near a month of their time, which had been much better spent in prosecuting their voyage to China. However, by the beginning of September, they reached the coast of China, where meeting with a typhoon, or a northeast storm that often blows violently about that season, they were forced to bear away for Johor, where they stayed about two months, and then came to Malacca, where they had a mind to clean their ship's bottom, and to proceed next April or May for China.

The Dutch received them civilly, and gave them leave to lay their ship ashore on an island to the westward of the town[1], about two or three miles from the fort, and allowed them to land their cargo and stores on the island till their ship was made clean, which they had perfected in two springs[2], and bringing the ship towards the road again, the captain being on board, ordered to steer the ship on some rocks that lay on the shore, and were dry at low water. The third mate, who was the only commanding officer on board except the captain, told him of the danger he was running into, and begged him to alter his course, but the captain cursed him for his impertinent advice, and ran the ship on the rocks, but the people got a small anchor and an hawser out, and brought her afloat again, but, as soon as the anchor was weighed, they ran her once more on the rocks, and she having a little motion, a rock worked itself through her

[1]   Pulau Upeh.
[2]   Tides.

bottom, and there she was lost without hopes or design of being recovered, and with her ended the Scots East India Company's interest in India. Whether the ship was lost by ignorance or design, I will not judge, but, in my opinion, it was by design, for, as I heard afterwards, the captain and supercargoes had taken up round sums on the bottom of the ship, and took that method to pay their debts. I came to Malacca about the beginning of August, and found the second supercargo in the ill state I have already mentioned, with the purser and the supercargo's writer, and eleven men more, who could not get passages to countries where they might get employment. I had then a great ship and a small one under my command, so I entered them all on board my ships in the same posts they had on board the *Speedwell*, and I entered on a scheme with the second supercargo to carry the Scots Company's effects on board my great ship to Scotland, but the first supercargo, who was before my arrival gone to China, and had no mind ever to see his native country again, broke our measures by rambling through India with his masters' stock. What the Scots Company's cargo was, I did not see; but the supercargoes had a chest of glassware in their own private adventure, the most obscenely shameful that ever I saw or heard of among merchants. They were priapuses[1] of a large size, with a scrotum big enough to hold an English pint of liquor, either to address the god Bacchus[2], or the goddess Venus[3], as seemed best to their votaries.

I prosecuted my voyage to Surat, and left the Scots supercargoes to pursue their masters' interest in getting

---

[1]   Penises. One can only speculate on the source of this glassware; the principal glass centres of Europe at the time were Venice and Bohemia, but there were many others.

[2]   The Roman god of wine and fertility.

[3]   The Roman goddess of love and beauty.

their affairs in a readiness to get a cargo for Europe, to be carried on board my ship according to an agreement made between the second supercargo and me. But, instead of putting affairs in a readiness, he embarrassed them, lent some of his masters' stock to some insolvent merchants in Amoy[1] in China, and let out some on the bottom of the ship he took his passage on board of, and though that ship was ordered by the owners and freighters back to Surat directly, a young gentleman, a supercargo, went with her to Bengal, and from thence to Persia, where the ship was seized by the owners' orders, and sent to Surat, where I met with the first supercargo half-dead with vexation for his folly, in keeping such a stock two years and an half without the least improvement: and what was left in China was in danger of ever [sic] being recovered, though it was afterwards.

At Surat the chief supercargo grew very weak, and, finding he had not long to stay in this world, had a mind to settle his affairs here before he went to the other, so one day he sent for me, to advise him what he should do with his masters' effects if he should die. I asked him if his accounts were brought forward, and he told me they were, and desired that I would take all into my possession, and be accountable to the Scots Company, and to remit it home to them, according to the orders they would send me about it. But I excused myself and would not meddle in their affairs on such weak terms; but I advised him to lodge his books and effects in the hands of one Mr Bernard Wyche[2], whom I took to be an honest and industrious gentleman; and so he did, and then he died.

He was a gentleman of a very courteous behaviour, and understood a small sword excellently well, but not much

---

[1]   Tsiamen in Fukien province, an important port which Hamilton visited several times.

[2]   The EIC's accountant in Surat in 1703.

versed in merchandise or foreign commerce. The second was a very good surgeon, and was master of the French language, but understood nothing in accounts. The captain, who stayed on board of my ship above twelve months, had been bred in his youth a driver of cattle from the highlands of Scotland into England. He had very mean education, and could not tell what he meant either in speaking or writing. He had a brutal courage, and was the husband of three wives all alive together. He knew nothing either of the theory or practical parts of navigation, and yet had been honoured with a commission for lieutenant in the Royal Navy of England.

I must now leave my long digression, and proceed from Malacca along the coast of Malaya, though there are no places of commerce between it and Johor Lama, which is sometimes the place of that king's residence, and has the benefit of a fine, deep, large river, which admits of two entrances into it. The smallest is from the westward, called by Europeans the Straits of Singapore, but by the natives Selat Tebrau[1]. It runs along the side of Singapore Island for five or six leagues together, and ends at the great river of Johor.

---

[1]   Hamilton writes Salleta de Brew for the old strait separating Singapore from the mainland.

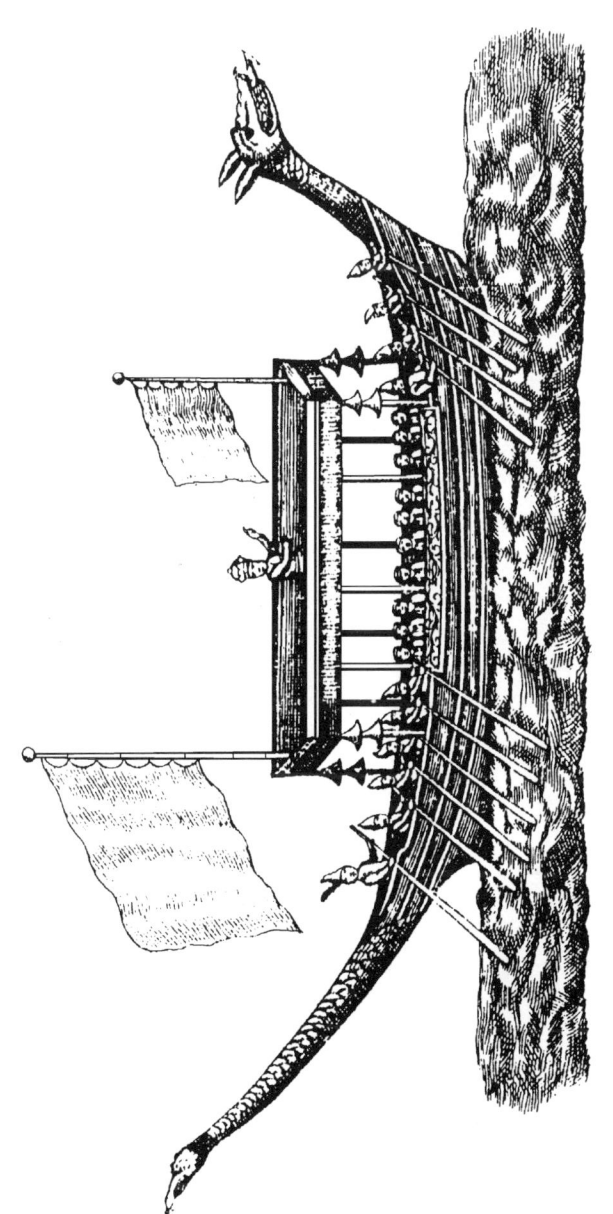

'A prospect of the King of Siam's pleasure Barge that he appears in on the River', again another sketch apparently of Hamilton's own pen.

Malay house, from T. and W. Daniell, Picturesque voyage to India by Way of China, 1810.

CHAPTER FIVE
[XL]

JOHOR AND ITS PALACE UPHEAVALS

T reats of the dominions of Johor, its ancient and present state occasioned by a revolution

The territories of Johor reached from Perak to Point Romano[1], which is the southernmost promontory on the continent of Asia, it lying but one degree to the northward of the equator, about three leagues from Johor River, in length about 100 leagues, and in the broadest place about eighty.

The inhabitants are lazy, indolent, perfidious and cruel. The country is very woody, being daily refreshed with showers and breezes of wind. It abounds in tin, pepper, elephants' teeth, gold, agala-wood and canes, but the inhabitants are such drones that they sow very little rice or other grain. And the inland people subsist mostly on sago, the pith of a small twig split and dried in the sun, and on their fruits which grow all seasons of the year, and roots, which they always have in great plenty, and poultry, which they rear up.

---

[1] Cape Romania.

About the sea coast they feed mostly on fish and rice brought to them from Java, Siam and Cambodia. The people of industry are the Chinese who inhabit among them in their towns; and there may be about 1,000 families of them settled in the Johor dominions, besides a much greater number who drive a foreign trade among them.

In religion they are heretical Muhammadans, and are supplied with priests from Surat; but the sayyids are in most esteem among them. They are great lovers of praying and preaching, and frequent their mosques very often, and look very devout; but their practices are the most irreligious and immoral of any people I know.

In Anno 1695 their king[1] was a youth of twenty years of age, and being viciously inclined, was so corrupted by adulation and flagitious[2] company that he became intolerable. I went to Johor Lama at that time, to traffic with his subjects and some Chinamen, with a cargo proper for their turn, and, according to custom, went to compliment His Majesty with a present, in which was a pair of screw-barrelled pistols. He desired me to prove them with a shot, to try how far it would penetrate a post that was at the gate, which I did, and he much admired how so little powder should have strength to force a ball so far in the wood, and begged some powder and ball, which I gave him, and the next time he went abroad, he tried on a poor fellow on the street how far they could carry a ball into his flesh, and shot him through the shoulder.

---

[1] Sultan Mahmud Shah II reigned from 1685 to 1699; in his early years his regents were his mother and Paduka Raja, who was driven out in 1688. Hamilton puts the date of his visit at 1695 but says on the next page that the sodomitic sultan was murdered "a year or two after I was gone"; it appears in fact to have been four years, if indeed he was there in 1695.

[2] Deeply criminal.

He was a great sodomite, and had taken many of his orang kaiya[1] or nobles' sons by force into his palace for that abominable service. A Moorish merchant, who was a freighter[2] on board my ship, had an handsome boy to his son, whom the king one day saw, and would needs have him for a catamite. He threatened the father that if he did not send him with good will, he would have him by force. The poor man had taken an house close by our ship, and immediately came with his son on board, imploring my protection, which I promised him. He had not been half an hour on board, till a guard came in a boat to demand him. I would suffer none to enter but the officer, and an interpreter for the Portuguese language[3]. The officer told me his errand, and, in an huffing manner, threatened me if I protected him[4]. I made him no answer, but taught him to leap into the river, and bid the interpreter tell the king that, if he offered the least violence to any that belonged to me, I would fire down his palace about his ears. He had never been contradicted before, much less threatened, and he sent for his orang kaiya to know if I was a king or no. They told him that I was on board of my ship, and that I would prove a dangerous enemy if provoked, and begged that His Majesty would remove to a village about twenty miles up the river, and stay till our ship was gone, which favour he willingly granted us, and so we traded with some more security, but were continually in arms for fear of a surprise.

He continued his insupportable tyranny and brutality for a year or two after I was gone, and his mother, to try if

---

[1] *orang kaiya* were literally wealthy persons; notables. Hamilton spells them 'Orankays'.
[2] A person who loads ships.
[3] Hamilton had clearly learnt Portuguese, thus following his advice given in his preface.
[4] i.e. the boy.

he could be broke off that unnatural custom of converse with males, persuaded a beautiful young woman to visit him when he was abed, which she did, and allured him with her embraces, but he was so far from being pleased with her conversation that he called his black guard, and made them break both her arms for offering to embrace his royal person. She cried, and said it was by his mother's order she came, but that was no excuse.

Next morning he sent a guard to bring her father's head, but he being an orang kaiya did not care to part with it, so the tyrant took a lance in his hand, and swore he would have it; but, as he was entering at the door, the orang kaiya passed a long lance through his heart, and so made an end of the beast.

The kingdom was three years without a king, but intestine discords daily arising, in Anno 1700 they chose another, a cousin german to him that was killed. His name was Sultan Abdul Jalil[1], a prince of great moderation and justice, and governed well for eight or nine years that he held the reins of government in his own hands. Trade flourished all over his dominions, and he was beloved by all his subjects, but being of a quiet disposition, and a great bigot to the Muhammadan religion, disposed himself to prayer and hearing sermons, and left the management of his government to a younger brother, called Raja Muda[2], a covetous tyrannical prince. The king never came out of his

---

[1] His full name was Sultan Abdul Jalil Riayat Shah IV, and he reigned from 1699 (not 1700) to 1718. His brother Tun Mas Anum was chief minister and in charge from 1699 to his death in 1708. Another brother, Raja Muda Indra Bungsu Tun Mahmud, then took over. Abdul Jalil was actually Mahmud Shah's last chief minister and reverted to this position in 1718, only to be killed by the Raja Kecil (of Siak) for plotting against him.

[2] Heir-apparent. His rule was tyrannous and he was overthrown in 1717 by Raja Kecil the ruler of Siak (Sumatra).

palace, but devoted himself wholly to the company of priests, who fed his mind with their nonsense and cant, and his brother keeping fair with the priests, came to oppress the people, and keep the king ignorant. I had the honour to be acquainted with him before he was king, and had free access to him when he was king; but his brother never suffered me to be alone with him, lest I should have discovered some of his evil practices, which I certainly had done if I could have found an opportunity, and to have forewarned him of the danger he was falling into. In Anno 1703 I called at Johor in my way to China, and he treated me very kindly, and made me a present of the island of Singapore, but I told him it could be of no use to a private person, though a proper place for a company to settle a colony on, lying in the centre of trade, and being accommodated with good rivers and safe harbours, so conveniently situated that all winds served shipping both to go out and come into those rivers[1]. The soil is black and fat, and the woods abound in good masts for shipping and timber for building. I have seen large beans growing wild in the woods, not inferior to the best in Europe for taste and beauty; and sugar cane five or six inches round growing wild also.

In 1708 the king's brother persuaded him to leave Johor Lama, and reside at Riau[2] on the island of Bintan[3], about three leagues off the river of Johor, because he thought he could act his tyranny with more security than on the main continent, and so at Riau he engrossed all trade in his own

---

[1] Singapore was to wait until 1819 before Raffles secured it from Temenggong Abdul Rahman of Johor.
[2] The Riau archipelago comprises numerous islands, of which Bintan is the largest. The Bugis, originating from southern Sulawasi, from 1722 ruled from there and the sultans of Johor were their puppets.
[3] South of Singapore.

hands, buying and selling at his own prices, and punishing those who dared to speak against his arbitrary dealings. At last, in 1712 a rebellion broke out, that nothing could stop but a revolution, which dissolved the state into anarchy.

Upon the rising of the people, the tyrant got on board of a galley, with his wives and children, and carried with him above a ton weight of gold, and, without taking leave of his brother, fled to Johor Lama, but finding a small army of Minangkabau[1] (whom the people had invited to their assistance) had taken their quarters there, he betook himself to the woods with his family, and left his galley and gold a prey to them. He knew that there could be no long safety in the woods, and despairing of mercy from the injured people, made desperation supply the place of courage. He first killed his wives and children, but began to hesitate about killing himself, but a page of twelve years of age asked him if he was afraid to die a prince rather than be butchered like a slave by some villain or slave's hand, and that he, though innocent, and who might expect mercy, would show him the way to die, and with that took a kris, and ran himself through the body. The tyrant presently followed the youth's example, and immediately expired; but the Minangkabau, coming soon after to the tragical place, saw what had been done, and found the boy alive, and in his senses. They stopped his bleeding wound, and carried him to Johor Lama till his strength returned.

When the king heard of the people's mutiny, and his brother's flight, he came out of his palace, and proffered to settle the state in its former tranquillity, and if that could not appease them, he thought nothing else could bring them to reason, but his life, which he would willingly sacrifice to atone for his maladministration.

[1]   Here, Malays.

The people told him that he was too religious to make a good king, and that he might retire to Pahang or Trengganu[1] and spend his time, but as for Johor and the islands between Sumatra and it, they would consider what to do with them, and so gave him some vessels to carry him and his family, with others who would follow his fortune, to Trengganu.

On his way thither, he called at Pulau Aor, Tinggi, Pisang and Tioman[2], and the inhabitants of those islands received him with demonstrations of love and promised to continue in their duty as his subjects. He put his eldest son[3], a youth about twenty years of age, ashore at Pahang, to keep that country from revolting, and went himself to Trengganu, where I afterwards had the honour to see him, and there I leave him at present, and return to those islands that lie round his dominions.

---

[1] Both are described later, in Chapter Eleven.
[2] A description of these islands follows in Chapter Eleven.
[3] He is named in Chapter Eleven as Rajah Bowncea, in Hamilton's spelling. Hamilton is possibly confusing Abdul Jalil's son with his brother Indra Bungsu; *bungsu* means 'youngest born' in Malay.

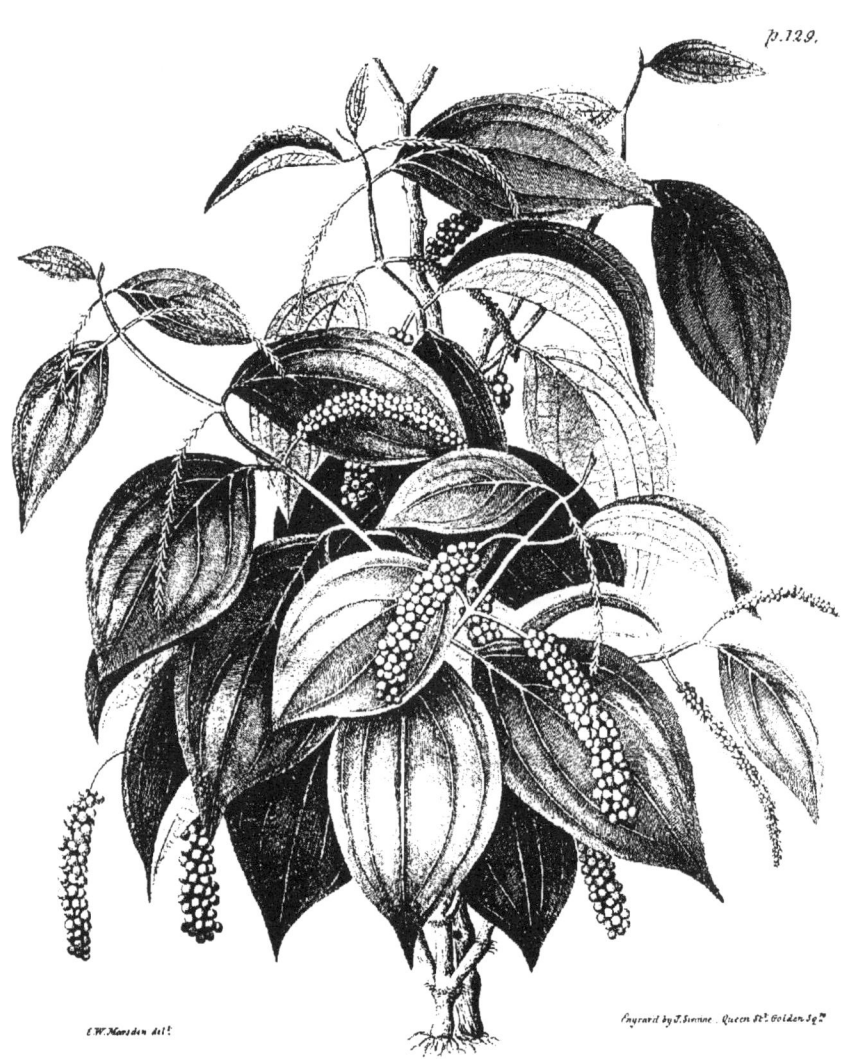

p.129.

THE **PEPPER-PLANT**, **PIPER NIGRUM**.

Published by W. Marsden, 1810.

The pepper plant, from Willian Marsden,
The History of Sumatra, 1810.

CHAPTER SIX
[XLI]

THE KINGDOM OF ACEH

G ives an account of the island of Sumatra, its places of note in trade

Sumatra fronts all the coast of Malaya, from Kedah to the promontory of Johor, and reaches above 150 leagues further. It is one of the greatest islands in the world. Aceh being the most conspicuous place for trade, I will begin with it, and coast along the west side of it, till I come round again to Andragiri, to the north-westward of which river there is little or no commerce.

Aceh for many ages has been a noted port for trade from Surat, Malabar, Cormandel, Bengal, Pegu and China. It lies at the northwest end of the famous Sumatra, and for many years was blessed with a woman's government. Queen Elizabeth of England sent the Queen of Aceh a compliment of some English rarities, among which were some brass guns[1], with the arms of England on them, and the friendship cultivated by the two queens procured great

---

[1] Foster dismisses this as a myth. A large brass gun was sent in the name of James I by the EIC in 1618 as a present to the Sultan of Aceh. The explorer Dampier heard that the palace contained four large guns from James I.

indulgences from the Queen of Aceh to the English who traded to her country. About the year 1675[1] the Dutch made war on her, because she would not permit them to settle a factory at Aceh, or rather, to make her their vassal. They shut up the port of Aceh by their shipping, and straightened the town for want of provisions and other necessaries that came yearly from Bengal. But an English ship came from thence with rice and cloth proper for the market; but the Dutch, after their usual manner, forbade the English traffic while they had a war. The master of the English ship being afraid of ruin by the loss of his voyage, sent advices to the Achinese to be ready near the shore on a night that he appointed, and he would run his ship ashore in the bay, loaded as she was, and they might have both the corn and cloth, whether the Dutch would or no, which project was put in practice, and had the desired effect, with the loss of the ship only. This piece of service so pleased the queen that she called a council of her orang kaiya, and magnifying the English friendship, in a full council declared all English free of Aceh, to pay for a ship with three masts, 100 taels[2], or about £80 sterling as a present to the queen, in lieu of all customs, let the cargo be never so rich, and for a brigantine or sloop forty taels, and that no English goods should be carried to the custom house, or surveyed in their own houses, and that all English merchants' houses were to be reckoned as sanctuaries to such as could not pay their debts or had committed any slight fault.

[1]   This is probably the blockade by Peiter de Bitter in 1664.

[2]   A weight used in East Asia (in Chinese a *liang*, one-sixteenth of a catty), roughly equal to an ounce; from this, a money of account, originally a tael in weight of standard silver.

This harmony continued till the year 1700 that the queen died[1], and a sayyid or preacher getting a strong party, was made king, promising to do wonders; but, in all my travels, I never found a civil government with a priest at the head of it prosper long, and so it fell out here. The first thing of moment he contrived was to make the English pay 10 per cent customs on the goods they imported, which they would not come into, nor would they unload their goods, but on the old footing.

In May 1702 I arrived there with a great ship and good force, for it was dangerous to traffic by sea, because of the impediment that the French[2] and the pirates gave to trade in India. I had on board a rich cargo from Surat, and on my arrival I took the chap[3] at the great river's mouth, according to custom. This chap is a piece of silver about eight ounces weight, made in form of a cross, but the cross part is very short, that we take with both hands and put to our forehead, and declare to the officer that brings the chap that we come on an honest design to trade, and after that ceremony is over we go in our boats freely to the town, which stands about four miles up the river; but, before we take the chap, no boat must go, on penalty of a fine.

When I came to town, I went to pay my visit to the shahbandar who is custom-master, and common arbitrator of differences arising among merchants. Some gentlemen

[1] The last queen of Aceh, Kamalat Syah Zinat ad-Din, died in 1699. She was succeeded by Badr al-Alam Syarif Hashim Jamal ad-Din (r.1699-1702), who represented the Arab element in Aceh, which suppressed female rule there.

[2] From 1701 to 1714 France was at war with Austria, England and the Netherlands over the Spanish succession.

[3] The Hindi original of 'chop', a term used in trade in the Indies and China, meaning a seal or its impression, or a mark used on goods and coins to indicate their nature or quality.

that resided there and some masters of ships belonging to the English accompanied me. I carried my boat's crew, armed with fusee[1] and bayonet, for my guard. After some compliments had passed between the shahbandar and me, he told me that if I had a mind to trade there I must carry my goods to the custom house, and there to be opened, and 10 per cent laid by for the king, whether we sold the rest there or no. I told him that was a new method that I did not understand, and could not come into, but withal advised him to take care how their king quarrelled with the English[2], who were as capable to reduce them to straits as the Dutch were, when the English relieved them. He answered me that they were not afraid of what the English could do, for their power being divided[3], they could do nothing but threaten.

I took my leave of him abruptly and told him that we knew how to fight in defence of our rights and privileges better than how to threaten. There were three English vessels lying in the river which had paid their customs and sold their cargoes at under rates, and two merchants that resided at Aceh. We all dined[4] together, and after dinner held a consultation how to behave in this affair that affected our merchants in general who traded thither. At last it was agreed that I should assist the merchants in getting their effects off on board of my ship, and to get their vessels out of the river, by the assistance of my boats and men, and

---

[1] Light musket or firelock.
[2] Hamilton is careful not to push his Scottish origin, though the Act of Union was not passed until 1707.
[3] The implication is not clear; perhaps it is a reference to the Indies being the preserve of a private company, possibly to the continuing friction between the Hanoverians and the Stuarts, or even the possibly over-extended distribution of the British colonial presence in North America and India as well as the East and West Indies.
[4] Lunched, in today's parlance.

then to shut up the port, all which was done in one day and a night. I then sent a linguist to tell the shahbandar that since the English were denied trade at their port, we forbade trade to any other nation, and desired that no boats might pass out of their rivers, either to trade or fish, on their peril. They continued quiet two days, and on the third they sent some boats off from a sandy bay about three miles from our ship. I sent two boats well manned to seize their nets but as soon as they perceived my boats, they ran theirs ashore, and took out what was in them; and as my boats were rowing near the shore within a mile of my ship, about forty or fifty muskets were fired on them out of some bushes that grow thick a little way from the strand. My boats fired in their turn at the place where they saw the smoke, and I made a signal to bring them aboard again, and found only two of my men slightly wounded.

The same evening we had advice that they were about mounting three culverins[1] that lay in a little fort on the river's side, as we go to town. I immediately ordered my armourer to get about 100 short spikes of several sizes, and harden them well, and carried them in my boat, which I double manned, and coming into the river we espied a great number of men in the fort. I rowed directly towards it, and they within expecting to have a message to carry to the king, stood gazing till we came close to the wall, and then we saluted them with a shower of twenty or thirty grenades that so frightened them that happy was he who got first away. We then entered the fort, and found some wounded men in it. We presently spiked up the vents of the guns, and left them, and came at our leisure aboard again.

A day or two after, as my boat was rowing along the shore towards a prau that was coming in towards the small river, they again fired out of their bushes. I had forty-two

[1] Small guns.

guns mounted on my ship, and bringing my broadside to bear, I got five-and-twenty on that side, and pointing them well among the trees and bushes where we observed the smoke to arise, we gave them a volley of great shot in return of their volley of small. By report our great shot did some execution, but particularly on the poor fishers, who had a village a little within the woods that we did not see.

This stoppage of trade and fishing, and killing and wounding the people, made a great noise among the poorer sort, having in nine days' time found more of the effects of hostility than ever they did in their lives before, and so, gathering together in great numbers, went in a body to the palace, threatening vengeance on the causers of their calamity, and if the English were not restored to their ancient privileges, they would have a woman to reign again.

A nephew of the deceased queen lived then privately at Pedir[1], a town about seven leagues off. Some orang kaiya who were discontented with the new king's government, first because he was a foreigner[2] and that the affairs of state were ill-managed, and that a war with the English was impending, wrote to that gentleman that if he would come to them with a small force, they would raise a party to dethrone him that reigned, and he might have a fair chance to succeed him.

However, the reigning king, not expecting that his new customs would meet with such opposition, sent an orang kaiya aboard of my ship with the linguist to know why we made war on him. We replied that he was the aggressor, by robbing us of our just rights and privileges acquired by our services, and in firing at our boats, so we wondered that the

---

[1] On the northeast coast of Sumatra.
[2] He was an Arab.

king could ask a reason of us. The orang kaiya told us that
he had brought a power[1] to make up all differences on the
king's part, but that we must consent to some new things,
as that we should pay no customs, but a present as before,
but that our goods must go to the custom house, and there
to be opened; and was going on, but I interrupted him, and
told him he had demanded more than could be granted
already, so he might save himself the trouble of making
further demands. When he found that nothing new could
be obtained, he said he would carry our answer to the king,
which he did; and the same evening proclamation was
cried through the streets that the English might again repair
to their respective houses, and trade on the old foundation.

Next day I went to wait on the shahbandar, but carried
a guard of twenty Europeans. He asked me why I carried so
many armed men in my company. I told him that I
understood there were like to be commotions in the
country, and I was resolved to be neuter, and would not be
insulted by either party. He begged that I would land some
bales of goods, to show that we were reconciled, which I
did, to the no small joy of the townspeople, who were quite
tired with their new king's experiments.

But the clamours of the people did not cease. For when
they had news of their deceased queen's nephew's raising
forces to come to Aceh, the disorders of the state increased,
but I left them, and pursured my voyage to Malacca and
Johor where I met with the Scots second supercargo, as is
before mentioned[2].

Aceh affords nothing of its own product fit for export,
but gold-dust, which they have pretty plentiful, and of the

---

[1]   Had the authority.
[2]   See text at p.63 note 1.

finest touch[1] of any in those parts, it being 2 per cent better than Indragiri[2] or Pahang gold[3], and is equal in touch to our guinea[4]. They do not dig for it, but catch it in gullies or little rivulets as it washes off the mountains, and one particularly, a very high mountain in form of a pyramid, called Gold Mount[5], which by report furnishes them yearly with above 1,000 pound weight.

Elephants are very plentiful at Aceh and consequently their teeth, which the Surat merchants buy up for their markets. In 1702 I saw one who had been kept there above 100 years, but by report was then 300 years old; he was about eleven foot high, and had a vast deal of sagacity.

When any young male elephant grows unruly, which they usually do in rutting time, and break their fetters and go astray, this old elephant is immediately sent out, and following the track of his foot, will find him out, and bring him back to his stable, either by fair or foul means.

At Aceh they have a small coin of leaden money called cash[6], from twelve to sixteen hundred of them goes to one mace[7], or masscie. The masscie is a small gold coin of 14 pence current, but in value about 12 pence English. I have taken a gold masscie, and put it with a masscie of cash, and thrown them into a puddle of water, and the elephant

---

[1]   Carat.
[2]   A formerly important state in east Sumatra, replaced by the trading centre of Siak, mentioned below.
[3]   From the east coast of Malaya.
[4]   The British gold coin, of 21 shillings in value.
[5]   Some 10 km from Aceh.
[6]   The term was common in the Far East, referring to an East Indian or Chinese coin; the word derives from Portuguese *caixa* which itself comes from the Tamil *kasu*.
[7]   The *Shorter Oxford Dictionary* gives for this "a weight and money of account equal to one tenth of a tael."

would find out the gold among the lead by the nice feeling of his proboscis.

There is a very comical piece of revenge he took on a taylor in Anno 1692. A ship called the *Dorothy*[1], commanded by Captain Thwaites, called at Aceh for refreshments in her way from England to Bengal, and two English gentlemen residing then at Aceh went aboard to furnish themselves with what European necessaries they had occasion for and, amongst other things, they bought some Norwich stuffs for clothes, and there being no English tailor to be had, they employed a Surat tailor, who kept a shop on the bazaar, or great market-place, and had generally half a dozen, or half a score workmen to sew in his shop. It was the old elephant's custom to reach in his trunk at doors or windows as he passed along the side of a street, begging decayed fruits or roots, which the inhabitants generally gave him.

As he was one morning going to the river to be washed, with his cornac[2] or rider on his back, he chanced to put his trunk in at the tailor's window, and the tailor pricked him with his needle, instead of giving an alms. The elephant seemed to take no notice of the affront, but went calmly on to the river and was washed, and being done with washing, troubled the water with one of his forefeet, and then sucked up a good quantity of that dirty water into his trunk, and passing unconcernedly along the same side of the street where the tailor's shop was, he put in his trunk at the window, and blew his nose on the tailor with such a force and quantity of water, that the poor tailor and his

---

[1] The ship, captained by James Thwaites, left England in 1691, reached Madras in May 1692 and departed for England again in October.
[2] Mahout. Cornac is the standard term in French, deriving from Sinhala; mahout is of Hindi origin.

lifeguard[1] were blown off the table they wrought on, almost frightened out of their senses, but the English gentlemen had their clothes spoiled by the elephant's comical but innocent revenge[2].

No place in the world punishes theft with greater severity than Aceh, and yet robberies and murders are more frequent there than in any other place. For the first fault, if the theft do not amount to a tael value, it is but the loss of an hand or a foot, and the criminal may choose which he will part with; and if caught a second time, the same punishment and loss is used, but the third time, or if they steal five tael in value, that crime entitles them to soweling[3], or impaling alive. When their hand or foot is to be cut off, they have a block with a broad hatchet fixed in it with the edge upwards, on which the limb is laid, and struck on with a wooden mallet, till the amputation is made, and they have an hollow bamboo, or Indian cane, ready to put the stump in, and stopped about with rags or moss, to keep the blood from coming out, and are set in a conspicuous place for travellers to gaze on, who generally bestow a little spittle in a pot, being what is produced by the mastication of betel, and that serves them instead of salve[4] to cure their wounds.

Those who suffer the penalty of the law who have no families in the town are banished to Pulau Wey, an island about four leagues to the north-eastward of Aceh, and there they cultivate the ground, and breed poultry for the use of

---

[1] His assistant or possibly his thimble.
[2] This story must have done the rounds of Southeast Asia with variations according to locale. The Chevalier de Forbin (1731, I. 126) has a very similar tale involving an elephant and a tailor set in Ayutthaya. Forbin claims to have seen this happen in 1685 or 1686.
[3] A sowel is a stake sharpened at one end.
[4] Healing ointment.

the town; and I have heard that there are above 500 of those bandit inhabitants on it. There is another island that lies about three leagues to the northward Pulau Wey[1] called Pulau Rondo. It is uninhabited, and sends forth a reef of rocks towards Pulau Wey, above one third part of the channel. Between them and Pulau Gomus[2] is a cluster of high mountainous and rocky islands, to the north-westward of Aceh and their end runs to seven leagues' distance from the road. There is no danger lying above a mile off them; and between Aceh Head, an high steep promontory, and the south end of Gomus Islands, there are two channels to come from the westward into the road. The smallest, which is not a quarter of a mile broad, has no danger in it, but the broadest, which is above two miles broad, is pestered with rocks half-way over from Gomus Islands.

The valleys about Aceh produce excellent fruits, and the best mangosteens in the world grow there. The air is very salutary, and the river waters are excellent for bathing. Washing in it before sunrising, and after setting, has cured inveterate fluxes[3]; and I have been told, that frequent bathing has cured the pox[4].

---

[1] Already mentioned in Chapter Three. Rondo is an islet close by.
[2] Pulau Kelapa, also mentioned in Chapter Three.
[3] Abnormal discharges from the body.
[4] Syphillis.

A MALAY,
native of Bencoolen.

Frontispiece

Published by W. Marsden, 1811.

A Malay native of Bencoolen, from Willian Marsden,
The History of Sumatra, *1810.*

CHAPTER SEVEN

WEST SUMATRA
[XLII]

G ives an account of the islands and trading ports on the west coast of Sumatra

And now I leave Aceh and pursue my travels along the west coast of Sumatra. Labuan[1] is the first place noted for gold-dust and camphor, but has no commerce with strangers. Hog Island[2] lies opposite to it, about ten leagues off. This island takes its name from the great numbers of wild hogs on it, who are the only inhabitants, as Coco Island[3], close to it, takes its name from the great numbers of coconut trees growing on it.

Barus[4] is the next place that abounds in gold, camphor, and benzoin, but admits of no foreign commerce. It lies within the south end of Hog's Island about the same distance from it that Labuan is. This place sets a boundary to the kingdom of Aceh.

---

[1] Labuan-haji, near Belangpidie.
[2] Pulau Babi; now renamed Simeulue.
[3] Two islands to the northwest of Simeulue.
[4] To the southwest of Lake Toba, opposite Nias.

Airbangis[1] is the next place of notice. It produces gold and pepper; it lies about 1 degree to the northward of the equator, and has the advantage of a good safe harbour, but it is little frequented, because of the treachery of the natives who make small account of murdering strangers if they can but get the least advantage by it. The harbour lies in a small but deep bay, and three small islands lying before it make it a most excellent harbour; and the channels between the islands, and between the shore and the islands, are clear of danger. The north end of Pulau Nias[2] lies about twenty leagues without it. The inhabitants of that island prove the best slaves in India, and are sold at an higher price in the Aceh market than any others.

Padang[3] is about twenty leagues to the southward of the equator, where the Dutch have a colony, and a strong fort to defend it from the insults of the natives. It cost the Dutch many men and much treasure before they could force a settlement there, though at last they gained their point, but being a country that produces only gold and pepper, the profits can hardly bear the charge. The island of Good Fortune[4] lies about twenty leagues without it.

Indrapura[5] is the next, and lies about fifty leagues to the southward of the equator. It was formerly an English factory, but the Dutch insulted[6] it in King William's war

[1] Some 100 km north of Padang.
[2] A large island to the west of Sumatra.
[3] The chief Dutch settlement on the west coast of Sumatra.
[4] Marsden (1783) gives the alternative name Si-porah (now Sipora); it is not Siberut, as Foster states, which Marsden has as 'Si-biru or Mantawei proper', and which curiously Hamilton does not mention in his text, though it appears on his map as smaller than Sipora.
[5] Marsden (1783) says this was a former kingdom with European settlers, all massacred in 1701, and which "dwindled into obscurity" in the early eighteenth century.
[6] Damaged, attacked.

with France[1] and it has made but a sorry figure in trade since. Its commodity is only pepper, but it affords great plenty of it, and very cheap. The island of Nassau[2] lies about fifteen leagues without it.

Bencoolen[3] is an English colony, but the European inhabitants not very numerous. About the year 1690 the East India Company built a fort there, and called it York Fort, but brick or stone walls in that country cannot long continue firm, because concussions of the earth are so frequent by earthquakes that solid walls are rent by the shaking of their foundations. It had the conveniency of a river to bring their pepper out of the inland countries, but great inconveniencies in shipping it off on board the ships, for there is a dangerous bar at the river's mouth, which has proved fatal to many poor Englishmen. The road for shipping is also inconvenient; for in the southwest monsoons, there being nothing to keep the great swell of

[1] William III, Prince of Orange, stadholder of the Netherlands, became King of England, Scotland and Ireland in 1689, reigning jointly with his wife Mary II. He brought England into the Grand Alliance (a coalition of the League of Augsburg, the Netherlands, Savoy and England) against Louis XIV in 1689-97, having already fought the French from 1672 to 1678. The Peace of Ryswick ended the War of the Grand Alliance, which was resumed as the War of the Spanish Succession, with the same belligerants, from 1701-1714. Since William III died in 1702, Hamilton must be referring to the Grand Alliance War.

[2] Marsden gives Pulao Pagi as the alternative name; these constitute North and South Pagai today.

[3] Bengkulu, where the English established a factory in 1684 and built a fort, was never profitable and always unhealthy; an 1805 report of the Fourth Presidency (Penang) declared it politically and commercially valueless. Marsden was at post there 1771-79 and Raffles at what he called "this miserable poor place" from 1818 to 1822, and again from 1823 to 1824, when under the Anglo-Dutch agreement it was exchanged for Malacca and the Dutch settlements in India.

rolling seas off them but a small island called Rat Island[1]; the ships are ever in a violent motion while that monsoon lasts.

The inland princes are often at variance among themselves, and sometimes are troublesome to the trade of our colony, but as their wars are short, the English are in little danger by them. In the year 1693 there was a great mortality in the colony, the governor and his council all died in a short time after one another, and one Mr Sowdon[2] being the eldest factor, had his residence at Prayman, or Priaman, a subordinate factory to Bencoolen, being called to the government of the colony, but not very fit for that charge, because of his intemperate drinking, it fortuned in his short reign that four princes differed, and rather than run into acts of hostility, referred their differences to the arbitriment of the English governor, and came to the fort with their plea. Mr Sowdon soon determined their differences in favours of the two that complained; and because the others seemed dissatisfied with his determination, ordered both their heads to be struck off, which ended their disputes effectually, and made them afterwards to make up differences among themselves without troubling the English with their contentions and impertinent quarrels; but governor Sowdon was sent for to Fort St George, and another sent in his place less sanguine.

And ever since that time there has been a succession of moderate governors, and some have been guilty of as

---

[1]   Pulau Tikus, just offshore.
[2]   Foster notes "Hamilton is not quite right in his facts." The head of the English settlement was Benjamin Bloom, who died in May 1680, and he was replaced by his senior assistant, James Sowdon. He was summoned to Madras because of numerous complaints against him and replaced by Charles Fleetwood.

much temerity the other way. For in Anno 1719 the then governor, having some disputes with some of the natives, was somewhat fearful of them. On a festival day, in firing guns, a wad from one of them set fire to an house thatched with reeds, and several others contiguous to it took fire from it, so that it spread through the market-place. The governor, believing it to be done maliciously by the natives, left the fort precipitantly, and got on board of a ship in the road, leaving some chests of money and all the artillery, arms, ammunition, and other effects of his masters behind him, and his garrison, following their leader, left their posts and got aboard also[1].

The natives, being surprised with the sudden departure of the English, went into the fort, and took what they had most occasion for; but some Chinese merchants, who had settled at Bencoolen, being also frightened, embarked on their vessels, and dispersed themselves in places where they thought they might be most secure.

The chief merchant of the Chinese, who is generally called the China captain in the places where the Chinese have trade, went to Batavia to some relations he had there, but the Dutch, according to their wonted hospitality in India, punished him as a criminal, and taught him to make lime and carry stones the remnant of his days for daring to settle among the English. Some of the Chinese I saw the same year at Trengganu in Johor who gave me this account. Wherever these poor Chinese came in places where the Dutch had power, they were as heartily persecuted as a poor Protestant is that takes sanctuary in a country where the holy, charitable, zealous Romish clergy have power.

---

[1]   Hamilton again gets his facts wrong. There was a native attack on the fort in 1719 and Thomas Cook, the chief at Bencoolen, and other survivors left for Batavia.

The natives were almost ruined by the English desertion. For as their trade lay all on their pepper, none came to buy it, and their regret being known at Fort St George, there was a new governor sent back with a new garrison, to take possession again of their own fort[1]. What the Company lost by that unaccountable piece of temerity, I know not, but they gained very little credit by it.

The country above Bencoolen is mountainous and woody, and I have heard that there are many volcanoes in this island; but whatever may be the cause, the air is full of malignant vapours, and the mountains are continually clothed with thick heavy clouds that break out in lightning, thunder, rain, and short-lived storms. Their food is not fit for every stomach. Tame buffalo may be had, but no cow-beef. Poultry are scarce and dear, and so is fish, but some sorts of fruits are pretty plentiful; however, the gentlemen there live as merrily, though not so long, as in other places blessed with plenty, and so sociable that they leave their estates to the longest liver.

Sillebar[2] lies but four leagues to the south-eastward of Bencoolen and has a fine convenient harbour to shelter shipping from all dangers caused by storms, but the fresh water is bad, and if drunk any considerable time causes gripings and fluxes; but it wants a river to bring pepper from the inland countries. There is no place of commerce or note between Sillebar and Lampung Point[3], which is the southwardmost point on Sumatra, nor anything remarkable on the seashore, but a small village called Pisang[4], which

---

[1] Bencoolen was reoccupied in 1721 or 1722 by Isaac Pyke, made chief of the west coast for the EIC's trade in Sumatra.
[2] Perhaps Marsden's Salumah.
[3] In Marsden's map this is named Flat Point.
[4] Marsden marks a small island, Pulao Pisang, close to the shore.

has a small low island lying a little way off it, and there is above forty fathoms deep within an English mile of the shore. And the island of Enggano[1] lies in the offing[2], about twenty leagues from it. It is an island about three leagues long, uninhabited, very smooth, without mountains, and may be seen nine or ten leagues off.

Lampung lies twenty leagues from the point within the Straits of Sunda, at the bottom of a deep bay. The English had a good pepper factory there, but it being a part of the King of Bantam's dominions, that factory was lost when the Dutch compelled the English to leave Bantam, in Anno 1683[3] and what Lampung produces is carried to them at Bantam.

[1]   Some 100 km to the west of Benkulu, named by the Portuguese on 1593 as the island of deception. It is now inhabited by five distinct animistic tribes.

[2]   Visible from the shore or anchoring ground.

[3]   1682. For Bantam, see Chapter Nine.

A plantation house in Sumatra, from Willian Marsden,
The History of Sumatra, *1810.*

EAST SUMATRA

Treats of the east side of Sumatra, with the adjacent islands, their product[s], commerce, and customs

There are no other places of note on that part of the Sumatra coast till we come to Palembang[1] which lies opposite to the northwest point of the island of Bangka[2] about four leagues distant from it. Palembang is a Dutch factory that brings them great quantities of pepper, being under contract with the King of Palembang and other inland princes to take off all their pepper at a certain price. I think it is for ten pieces of eight, or 50 shillings sterling a bahar[3], of 400 pounds English suttle weight[4], one half to be paid in money, and the other half in cloth. The cloth part the company pays at 70 per cent on the prime cost; but all other nations are debarred commerce there, except the

---

[1]   This ancient capital of the Srivichaya kingdom lies 80 km upstream from the coast. The Dutch fort survives.
[2]   Bangka was famous for its tin; it is described more fully in the pages which follow.
[3]   The *Shorter Oxford Dictionary* defines this as "a measure of weight used in India China, varying in different places from 223 to 625 lbs."
[4]   After the deduction of tare, the weight of packing or wrapping.

Chinese, and by their means the English come in for a share of their pepper, as our ships pass through the Straits of Bangka.

Palembang lies about eight leagues from the sea, on the banks of a large river[1], which divides itself into several branches, and they disembogue [sic] at four mouths into the sea. The Dutch keep two small sloops cruising about those mouths of the river, to prevent smuggling, but I and many others have found ways and means to lade our ships full with pepper, notwithstanding the strict guard. An hundred pounds to the king, and as much to the Dutch chief, make a cargo of a 1,000 bahars easily procured.

The Palembang pepper is very foul, insomuch that we seldom find less than 10 or 12 per cent garblage[2], but then we buy it for 9 pieces of eight a bahar. The Dutch lade off about 3,000 tons per annum from this place, and the Chinese and natives lade off as much more. The natives are obliged to carry theirs to Batavia, and sell to the Dutch Company, but if they meet with a market by the way, they'll embrace it; for the Company's payment being most in cloth at high rates, they are not fond of trading with them[3].

The Dutch Company formerly drove a good trade in opium at Palembang which (like French claret and brandy) drew much ready cash out of his country, as those do out of ours, but in Anno 1708 the king ordered only the importation of three chests, each containing about 160 pound weight, and if smugglers were detected, they paid their goods and lives for their disobedience.

---

[1] The Musi.
[2] Refuse after sifting.
[3] The consequences of the VOC's policy of 'buy cheap, sell dear' are clearly seen here.

The island of Bangka lying so near the coast of Palembang, I'll take a view of it as I pass along. It is about fifty leagues long, and sixteen broad, some places being broader, and some narrower. For about thirty leagues it faces the Sumatra coast, keeping between three and six leagues distant. The entrance from the southward being farthest distant in the Straits of Bangka, at the mouth of which is the island of Lucipara[1], a small barren island, which sends forth sandbanks almost three leagues towards the coast of Sumatra. And within a mile of that shore, where the channel is deepest, there are but four fathoms and an half water, but the bottom is soft.

About twelve leagues from the north end is the place of the king's residence. In 1710 a son of the King of Palembang was king, and a fire accidentally happening in a village, when the fire was extinguished, they chanced to find much melted metal under the rubbish, which proved to be tin. The king ordered his people to dig a little into the ground, and they found plenty of ore, which he now reaps a good advantage by. The Dutch sent from Batavia for leave to settle a factory there, but could not obtain that favour, the king declaring that his country should be free for all nations to trade in.

The natives of the island are, as most other Malays, very treacherous, inhumane and inhospitable to strangers who have the misfortune to be shipwrecked on that coast. I knew one Captain Pelling, who belonged to some gentlemen of Aceh and had the misfortune to be shipwrecked there, and they cut him off and all his crew, except two boys who were made slaves: but I know a very honest ingenious gentleman now alive in England who had better fortune, for, after his ship was lost in the Straits of

---

[1] At the southern end of the Bangka Straits, it was the cause of numerous groundings.

Bangka, he and his men directed their course to Palembang, where a very hospitable Dutch gentleman, who fortuned to be chief of the Dutch affairs at that time, gave them a kind reception, and procured them passage for Batavia, where, some years after, I was in company with the host and guest together.

Bangka has a very foul coast for six leagues within Manumbung Point[1], which is the northwest capeland on the island: and over that cape there is an high mountain called Manumbung Hill. On the northeast coast of the island there are so many banks and rocks under water that navigation is very precarious, and none but panjalangs[2] and praus (small vessels) venture to go that tract; besides, there are no places of commerce on the northeast side of Bangka to invite a stranger by the prospect of gain, and so I return back to the coast of Sumatra again, without taking notice of the little pepper and damar[3] that are the product of Bangka.

From Palembang there are no places of commerce on the coast till we come to Jambi[4], which is about 100 English miles. Here formerly the English had a factory on an island near its river's mouth, called Berhala[5]; but the impediments their trade met with from the Dutch, who had a factory in the country up the river, made the English company withdraw[6]. The Dutch kept a little factory at Jambi till 1710

---

[1]   Hamilton calls this 'Monapin' and Marsden 'Monopin'; it is close to the modern Muntok.
[2]   Small native boats.
[3]   Resins and tree gums.
[4]   Jambi was a dependency of Java's Majapahit empire from 1294 to 1520 and then came under the Minangkabau of West Sumatra. The EIC opened an office there in 1616.
[5]   Sometimes Varella; Hamilton writes 'Barella'.
[6]   The EIC withdrew in 1680-1.

and then withdrew also[1]. That country produces only pepper and canes; and, by the laziness of the inhabitants, there is hardly any of them procurable.

The island Lingga[2] lies under the equator, about twenty leagues from Jambi, and as far from the river of Johor, and is a part of the Johor[3] dominions. It is about twenty leagues long, and ten broad. It is very mountainous within, and very low towards the sea. Its product is some pepper and canes, and it abounds in porcupines, which affords them the valuable porcupine bezoar[4]. Some of them I have seen as big as a walnut, and of the same shape, and pretty near in colour, valued at 600 pieces of eight. Between Lingga and Sumatra are the Straits of Durians[5], where generally ships pass that go from Malacca to Batavia.

On the Sumatra shore there are no places of commerce till we come to the south entrance of Indragiri River[6], and there lies Pattapan[7], a town belonging to the dominions of Johor, that affords pepper and gold. Off the mouth of that river about ten leagues lie the two islands of Karimun[8], and between them and the Sumatra shore are the Straits of Labon[9]. Upon the east side of the great Karimun is the entrance of the Straits of Durians; and between the small

---

[1] The Dutch founded their factory in 1670; it is mentioned by Valentyn as still existing in 1724.
[2] Lingga and its southern island, Singkep, are part of the Riau archipelago. The Berhala Strait separates Singkep from Sumatra.
[3] Described in Chapters Five and Eleven.
[4] A stone from an animal's stomach, held to have medicinal properties.
[5] Hamilton's 'Drion' Strait is to the north of Lingga.
[6] Marsden named this river as one of the great rivers of Sumatra.
[7] Untraced. Marsden marks nothing to the south of the Indragiri, but Muara Besar to the north.
[8] The Great and Lesser Karimun islands lie between Sumatra and Singapore.
[9] Not marked in modern maps, nor that of Marsden.

Karimun and Tanjung Bulus[1] on the continent is the entrance of the Straits of Singapore[2] before mentioned, and also into the Straits of Governadore[3], the largest and easiest passage into the China Seas. There are many islands lying thick hereabout, all under the dominions of Johor.

The Dutch have also a factory on the river of Indragiri, called Siak[4], but of no great moment. It is so unhealthful that incorrigible sots, and other lumber of the active world, are sent thither to expiate their offences against nature, and very seldom any return back to give an account of the salubrity of the country. The reason may be that yearly there are vast numbers of fish called shades, about the bigness of a large haddock, full of bones, and roes about one third of their own magnitude, which come into that river to spawn, and great numbers of people resort thither in that season to catch them for the sake of their roes, and throw away the rest of the fish, which so corrupts the air that few can hold out one year, but are relieved every six months, except those who are sent for sacrifices to Pluto[5].

The Dutch have another factory right opposite to Malacca, on the side of a large river, called Benkalis[6]. Whether that be a branch of Indragiri River I know not, but I believe it is. The company vends a great deal of cloth and opium there, and brings gold-dust in return. That beneficial

---

[1]   The southernmost point of the Malay peninsula; Marsden has Tanjong Bulan.
[2]   The old channel to the north of the island.
[3]   The modern Singapore Straits.
[4]   Siak lies upstream on the Siak or Sugu River, not the Indragiri. Modern maps sometimes also refer to it as Sri Indrapura, after an early kingdom which was taken over by Aceh.
[5]   The Roman god of the underworld.
[6]   Benkalis Island, Marsden's Pulo Panchor, lies southwest of Malacca. The settlement is on the southern side of the island.

trade was not known to the Dutch before 1685 that one Mr Lucas, a factor in the company's service at Malacca, was advised by a Malay to send some Surat baftas dyed blue, and some berams[1] dyed red, which are both coarse cotton cloth much worn in that country; and opium is as much in request there as tea is with us. In ten years that he kept that trade wholly to himself, though in other men's names, he got an estate of ten or twelve tons of gold, or about 100,000 pounds English, and then revealed the secret to the Company, who took that trade altogether into their own hands.

There are prodigious numbers of wild swine about Benkalis, and in the months of December and January their flesh is very sweet and fat. In those months great numbers of people resort thither in small praus. Some go into the woods, and drive them towards the river, while others are ready with dogs to drive them into it, and when one goes, all the herd follows. Others are ready with lances in their praus to pursue them in the water and lance them, and so many as are lanced drop down on the other shore, and they are immediately carried to places appointed, where there are many fires made of brushwood and leaves of trees, which the woods afford in great plenty, and in those light flames they singe the hair off, and take out the entrails, and cut them up in proper pieces, and salt them in the praus; and every prau had a share proportionable to the number of men it brings. After it has lain three or four days in salt, they wash the pork, and hang it in smoke, and then put it into casks, which they have ready for their purpose, with some dry salt, and sell it by the cask to the best bidder. And I think it is the most savoury salt pork that ever I tasted.

---

[1] 'Surat baftas... and some berams'. As explained here, coarse cotton cloth, the former originating from Surat in India.

Those fish roes caught at Siak, they pickle up in salt and tamarinds, and then dry them in smoke, and when dry enough, put them up in large leaves of trees, and transport them to all the countries about, from Aceh to Siam. It is called, when dried, turbow[1], and of pork and turbow they drive a good trade, which, I think, far exceeds caviar.

There is no other place on the Sumatra coast between Bengkalis and Aceh that admits of commerce with strangers, though there are several large rivers; at least by their outlets to the sea, they appear to be so. There is one called Deli[2] that lies five leagues within Pulau Varela[3], a small uninhabited island that affords nothing but fresh water and wood. The inhabitants on that part of Sumatra are said to be cannibals[4]. Diamond Point[5] lies about twenty leagues to the northwest of Pulau Varela, that sends dangerous rocks above a league off shore. The inhabitants are uncivilized, murdering all whom they can surprise or master. And at Pisang[6], about ten leagues to the westward of Diamond Point, there is a fine deep river, but not frequented, because of the treachery and bloody disposition of the natives. Twelve leagues farther west lies Pedir[7]. It has the benefit of a good river, but being but eight leagues from Aceh, it has no trade.

[1]   Trubu, a fish similar in habits to the salmon.
[2]   The seat of the sultanate of Deli is modern Medan, on the Deli River. It was embroiled in a power struggle with Aceh throughout the seventeenth century.
[3]   East of Medan.
[4]   This undoubtedly refers to the Bataks.
[5]   Jambu Ayer or Jambuair.
[6]   Passanga.
[7]   Marsden's Pidir, previously mentioned in p. 86 note 1.

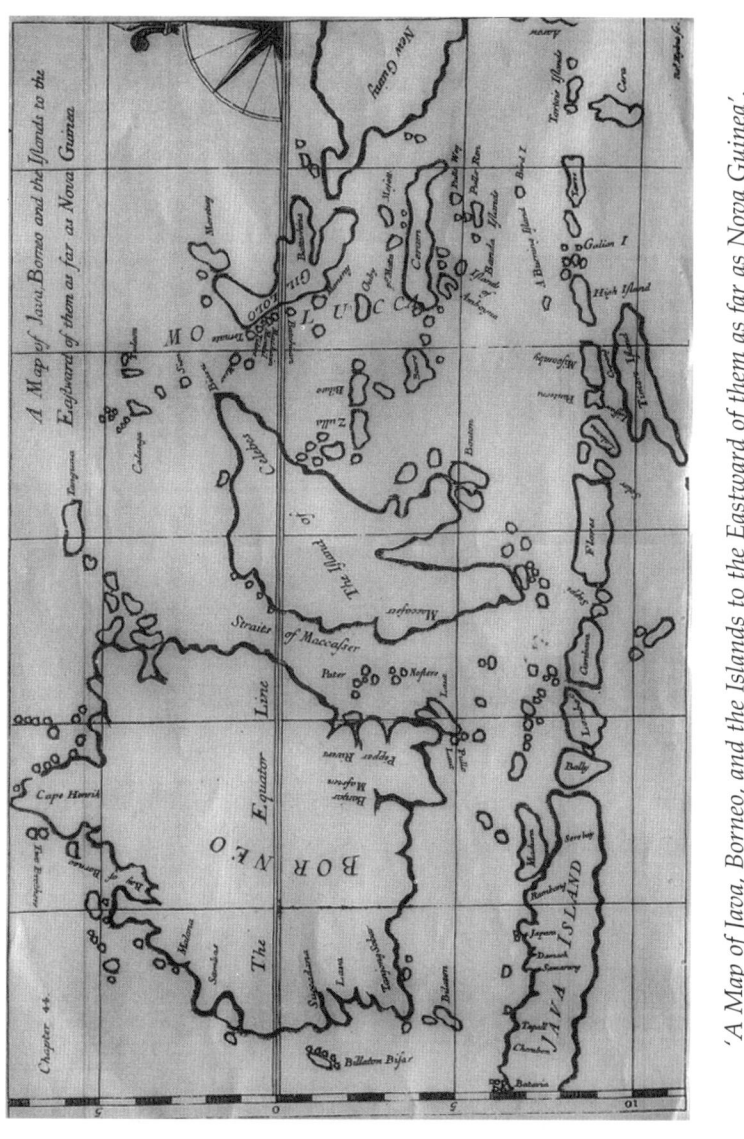

'A Map of Java, Borneo, and the Islands to the Eastward of them as far as Nova Guinea'.

A Javan of the lower class,
from T.S. Raffles, The History of Java, *1817.*

CHAPTER NINE
[XLIV]

JAVA AND THE EASTERN ISLANDS

Treats of Java, and the islands near it, with an account of the garrisons and factories settled on that island by the Dutch, the product and commerce of Java, Bali, Lombok, Flores, Solor, Lomblen, Pantar, Alor, Timor, Banda and Molucca islands, and the islands of Celebes, their product[s], extent and commerce

And now having ended my tour round Sumatra, I must return to the southward, and travel to the eastward of Sumatra, and to the southward of the equator, among those famous islands; and Java being the westmost, I begin there, and march eastward among islands far from any continent.

Princes Island[1] is close to the west point of Java. It has a channel between it and Java, but there is some danger in it. There are no inhabitants on it; but there are three places that afford good water, and wood enough for ships bound out of the Straits of Sunda to Europe. There are several

---

[1]   Panaitan.

other islands in the straits, as Krakatoa[1], Duars in the Way[2], the Button[3] and Cap[4], and several others without name.

The first place of commerce on the west end of Java is the famous Bantam, where the English and Danes had their factories flourishing till Anno 1682, at which time the neighbourly Dutch fomented a war between the old King of Bantam and his son, and because the father would not come into their measures and be their humble slave, they struck in with the son, who was more covetous of a crown than of wisdom[5]. They, with the assistance of other rebels, put the son on the throne, and took the old king prisoner, and sent him to Batavia; and, in 1683 they pretended a

[1] This is the famous volcano that blew itself up in 1883. Hamilton makes no mention of 'Emperor Island', Pulau Tabuan, mentioned by Chaumont and Choisy in their journey in 1685 through the straits and marked in Placide's map of 1686.

[2] A translation of the Dutch Dwars in den Weg, Sungian Island, in the middle of the strait, splitting it into two channels.

[3] Foster gives an alternative name of Toppers for this island.

[4] Also known as Pulau Ulas.

[5] The sultanate of Bantam (also spelt Bantem and Banten) enjoyed a thriving trade with Portuguese Malacca. Sultan Ageng acceeded to the throne in 1651 and Bantam became the centre of English trading activities in the archipelago; it was placed dangerously close to Batavia, a Dutch colony since 1619. The sultan carried out considerable agricultural extension works and retired to the village of Tirtayasa in 1678, handing the kingdom over to his son, Sultan Haji, who murdered his father's close advisors and chief minister. The popular Sultan Ageng decided to reassume power. His son took refuge in the fortress and managed to get a message to the Dutch in Batavia. They sent ships to help him and a civil war occurred. Sultan Ageng and his followers took refuge outside the town in the face of Dutch troops, and were forced to capitulate; Ageng was taken prisoner in 1682 and incarcerated in Batavia, where he died. The Dutch demanded in recompense that Sultan Haji expel all foreigners from Bantam, installed troops in the town and the palace, and exercised a monopoly over the pepper trade. Thereafter Bantam was in complete decline.

power from the new king to send the English and Danes apacking, which they did with a great deal of insolence, according to custom. They next fortified, by building a strong fort within a pistol-shot of one that the old king had built before to bridle their insolence.

The only product of Bantam is pepper, wherein it abounds so much that they can export 10,000 tons per annum. The road is good, and secure for the safety of shipping. It is in a pleasant bay wherein are several small islands which retain their English names still; and the natives still lament the loss of the English trade among them, but the king has much more reason than his subjects to regret the loss of their commerce. The goodwill the natives bear to the Dutch may be conjectured from their treatment, when they find an opportunity, for if an Hollander goes but a musket-shot from their fort, it is five to one if ever he returns, for they are dextrous in throwing a lance, or shooting of poisoned darts through a wooden pipe or trunk; and the king never redresses them, pretending the criminal cannot be found.

Batavia is about twenty leagues to the eastward of Bantam, and a great number of small islands lie scattered in the way, too tedious to mention[1]. Pulau Panjang[2] off Bantam, and Edam[3] off Batavia are the most conspicuous, and the road of Batavia[4] is almost surrounded with islands,

---

[1] Outside Batavia (Jakarta) are the Seribu Islands (literally one thousand), in fact numbering 112.

[2] This island lies in the centre of the Bay of Bantam.

[3] Marked in Raffles' map of Java as Idam Is.

[4] Hamilton says remarkably little here about this most important centre of commerce, though it would be the most appropriate place. It had, of course, been frequently described by travellers, who were for the most part all mightily impressed by the magnificence on the Dutch Governor-General's court and the layout of the city. There is

some of them inhabited, and some not. Its topography I'll refer to another time, with some historical accounts of it, both ancient and modern.

Cirebon[1] is the next colony on the coast, to the eastward of Batavia, belonging to the Dutch, where they have a fort and a small garrison.

Tegal[2] is also a Dutch settlement, with a small fort for its defence; and there is no other remarkable place till we come to Semarang[3], a good colony, with a fort of mud and wood to defend it. Demak[4] and Kudus[5], two places that lie between Semarang and Jepara, are noted, one for the abundance of rice that it exports, and the other for great quantities of good sugars that it produces. They are peopled mostly with Chinese, and so is Jepara[6], which

no further description of Batavia in these pages, though Hamilton makes several incidental references to trade or contact with the city, and in his discussion of the island of Flores below makes clear he had visited the city.

[1] The city was the seat of three sultanates and had enjoyed a prosperous trade with China until ceded to the Dutch in 1677 by Sultan Agung of Martaram. By a further treaty of 1705 it became a Dutch protectorate.

[2] Amangkurat I was buried here in 1677 after his flight from Plered.

[3] Semarang was ceded by Amangkurat II to the Dutch in 1677 in return for his recognition as Susuhan.

[4] The first Islamic state in Java, it was the most important place in Java in the early sixteenth century. Its mosque is the earliest in Java, built by the "nine wali" in 1478; the tomb of Sunan Kalijagga is a place of pilgrimage.

[5] Founded by an Muslim holy man, Sunan Kudus, whose tomb behind the main mosque, constructed in 1549, is a place of pilgrimage.

[6] The town had a history of violence between the Dutch and the Javanese. It was burnt down in 1618 by Coen along with the EIC's post. It was then for a time the VOC headquarters of the central north coast of Java but was forcibly closed by the Javanese in 1660. It is now more famous for its woodcarving than its sugar cakes.

formerly had an English factory, but now is altogether in the Dutch hands. It is defended by two forts, one on an hill, and the other in a plain, where the town stands, and has a small river to wash its walls. The road is secured by two islands that lie about a league off the town. I bought good white sugar in cakes here for two Dutch dollars per picul[1], being 140 lb. English suttle weight.

Tampeira[2] is the next place to the eastward, and to the eastward of it is Rembang[3], about two leagues from it, where the Dutch have a small wooden fort, and a little garrison of sixteen men. Those two afford nothing but excellent teak timber for building. And to the eastward of Rembang is Surabaya[4], which lies within[5] the island Madura[6], and, I believe, is the eastmost settlement the Dutch have on the island of Java. It produces much pepper, some beeswax and iron. Surabaya is about 125 leagues to the eastward of Batavia, and the country, alongshore, as pleasant and fruitful in grain and fruits as any in the world. Tame cattle and wild game are very plentiful, good and cheap. At Rembang I bought a cow, fleshy and fat, for 2 pieces of eight, that weighed above three hundredweight, and wild hog and deer we killed daily with our fowling-pieces, as we did also peacocks and wild poultry. The cocks

---

[1] A measure of weight used in East Asia, equal to 100 catties, as Hamilton says about 133.3 pounds avoirdupois.

[2] Perhaps modern Tayu.

[3] Rembang was the site of a massacre of the Dutch in 1741; it is now chiefly known for its Kartini museum.

[4] A powerful and rich state in the sixteenth century, and in the following century was taken by Sultan Agung. The Dutch occupied the city in 1706.

[5] Nearby.

[6] In the eighteenth century the island of Madura was ruled by the powerful Cakraningrat line, who were most often (though not always) allied to the Dutch.

are all like one another, with red necks and bodies, and black wings and tail; and the hens are exactly like large partridges. The cocks are pretty large, and when they take wing, they make a noise that may be heard half a mile. Their flesh is both savoury and juicy; and the wild hog is excellent. In the woods are many flying squirrels. Some of them I have seen tame in cages. They also have little horses wild in the woods, and some tigers, but being not much pinched with hunger, they seldom attack men. They have one dangerous little animal called a gecko[1], in shape almost like a lizard. It is very malicious, and pisses at everything that offends it, and wherever the liquor lights on an animal body, it presently cankers the flesh, unless immediate cauterizings are used, and if that cannot be had, the piece must be cut out for, if once it blisters the skin, there is no cure for it afterwards; but he seldom fails of giving notice where he is, by a loud noise calling 'gecko'.

I was once at supper with some Dutch gentlemen at Rembang, in an house thatched with coconut leaves, and we were no sooner set, but one of those geckos opened its throat almost over our heads. The Dutch gentlemen took the alarm, and arose from the table in great haste, and ran out of the room, calling to me, who sat still (not a little surprised to see their sudden flight) to follow them, for my life was in danger, and, on hearing that admonition, I was not long after them; but its noise spoiled our supper.

As there are many species of wild animals in those woods, there is one particular, called the orang-utan[2]. It is

---

[1]   The EIC agent Catchpole, in 1703, writing from Pulo Condore, gave its Thai name of *toukay* ("tockaie"). It is not venomous, but its grip cannot be easily released.

[2]   Literally, forest-man; these are not found in Java, but in Borneo and Sumatra.

nearest to human, both in shape and sagacity, among all the herd of animals. I saw one about four foot high, gross-bodied, long arms from the shoulders to the elbows. His finger ends reached just to his knees as he stood upright. His thighs and legs plump, but too small in proportion to his body. His feet long, and broad at the toes, but a little too narrow at the heel. His belly prominent, covered with a light-coloured fur, the rest of his body being brown, and the fur thicker and longer than the belly fur. His head somewhat large. His face broad and full. His eyes grey and small. His nose little and flat. His upper lip and underjaw very large. He blows his nose, and throws away the snot with his fingers, can kindle a fire, and blow it with his mouth. And I saw one broil a fish to eat with his boiled rice. The females have their regular menstrua. They have no tail, and walk upright. They are of a melancholy disposition, and have a grave dejected countenance, and even when they are young, they are never inclined to play, as most other animals are. There is a smaller sort, but of a different species, called oumpae[1]; but their legs and arms are very small.

They have many large crocodiles or alligators in their rivers and marshes, and sometimes they go a mile or two off to sea, and get foul of the fishers' nets. I was cleaning a vessel (that I bought at Semarang) on a bed of ooze, and had stages fitted for my people to stand on, when the water came round the vessel, and we were plagued with five or six alligators, which wanted to be on the stage, and every moment disturbed our men, so I and two of my men sat on the vessel's deck and fired muskets at them, but our ball did them no harm, because their hard scaly coat was shot-proof. At last we contrived to shoot at their eyes, and we

---

[1]   Ungka, or gibbon.

shot at one so. As soon as he found himself wounded, he turned tail on us, and, with great flouncings, made towards the shore about half a mile from us, and the rest following him. We were pretty quiet after that. A day or two after, some fishers told us that they had seen a dead alligator lying on the shore, and pointed whereabout they saw him. I went in a boat ashore, and found him lying at full length. I measured his length, and found, from his nose to his tail, twenty-seven foot and an half, and he was about one third part of his length in circumference about the belly.

I was in Semarang in 1704 in the months of July and August, when navigation on that coast is accounted dangerous. A war happened then to break out between the natives of that part of Java and the Dutch, about the succession of a new Susuhan or emperor[1], the old one demising about that time. The Dutch would impose the old emperor's brother on them against the general bent of the nation, and the nobility were for his eldest son, being the established law and custom of the country.

I being then bound for Batavia, the commodore desired me to carry a packet of letters for the general and his council, which I did, and delivered them, before they were

---

[1]   Emperor is the correct translation of this title of Mataram. Amangkurat II died in 1703. Hamilton muddles his facts; the Susuhan was succeeded by his bloodthirsty son Sunan Mas, Amangkurat III, and his uncle Prince Puger was supported by the Dutch, with whose help in the first Javanese War of Succession he occupied Kartasura and was installed as Pakubuwono I in 1705. In 1706 Amangkurat III surrendered to the Dutch and was sent into exile in Ceylon. But on the death of Pakubuwono I in 1719 the second Javanese War of Succession broke out and lasted four years before Pakubuwono's son Amangkurat IV was recognized by all his brothers. Hence Hamilton's comment about the length of the war a little further on.

six days old, to the general, Jan van Hoorn[1], which piece of service recommended me to his favour, which he demonstrated afterwards in some indulgences I had, and some confidence he reposed in me.

The war begun then lasted twenty years longer than at first the Dutch imagined. It taught the Javans the art of war, having a great number of Makassars[2] and Balinese[3], who had been trained up in the Dutch Company's wars against several nations. Many of them came into the eldest son's interest, who having as good courage and subtle stratagems, with much greater agility of body than the Dutch, made the war more terrible and dangerous than any the Company had ever entered into, notwithstanding the pretender had a large party of Javans, and was assisted by Makassars, Ambonese[4], Balinese and Bugis[5]; but they wanted the European discipline that the others had who served the young emperor, for they could encamp and mine as well as the Dutch.

A Dutch captain, in his march towards the Dutch camp, fell with his company into an ambush of Javans. Some of his men were killed, but he and most of his men were taken prisoners. The Dutch camp was pitched on the side of a river, and the Javans a few miles above them on the same river's side. Next day, to the Dutch great amazement, they saw the captain and his men swimming down with the stream, on bundles of reeds, with all their legs, thighbones and arms broken, and most of them alive. Their countrymen took them out of the river, and used means to save

---

[1] Van Hoorn was governor-general from 1704-1709.
[2] Inhabitants of the southern Celebes.
[3] Hamilton's 'Ballies', who formerly had a warlike reputation.
[4] For Ambon, see below, p.126 note 5.
[5] The Bugis came from the south of the Celebes.

their lives, but very few lived, which put their whole army in some dread, by observing what quarter they might expect if any of them were taken prisoners.

The religion of Java is partly Muhammadan and partly pagan[1]. The pagans choose women to be priestesses, and they are generally old, and well-skilled in witchcraft. And it is reported that they have frequent conversation with the devil, who appears to them in an horrid monstrous shape[2] and the priestesses sacrifice an hog to him. The emperor resides at an inland town called Kartasura[3] about three days journey from Semarang, where I'll leave him, and proceed to the island of Madura, that produces nothing for a foreign market but deer skins. They may be had in great abundance, and very cheap. This island confronts Java to its very easternmost point. I have no knowledge of the islands to the eastward of Java, but what I have had by information from the Dutch, who are the only possessors of that commerce, except two English ships that fell in among some of those islands, and so I will go on in those lame observations and remarks.

I observed before that Surabaya was the easternmost settlement the Dutch have on Java, neither have they any footing that I have heard of on the south side of that island, though the natives are pretty well civilized, and as ships from Europe fall in with that coast, they will bring off

---

[1]   Hamilton must be referring to the residual Hindu element still in East Java at this time. Balam-Bangan (Banyuwangi) in the easternmost part of the island remained under Hindu princes and did not fall to the Dutch until 1777.

[2]   This may be the Balinese barong.

[3]   This was established as the seat of the court of Martaram by Amangkurat II in 1680; after endless disasters Pakubuwono II decided to move the court to Surakarta, some 10 km to the east, in 1743; the move took place early in 1746.

provisions to sell them, particularly if they see English colours, for very often the Dutch buy their commodities, but pay nothing for them.

The island of Bali[1] lies next Java to the eastward. It abounds in provisions for the inhabitants, but affords nothing fit for exportation. The natives are daring and bold, even to desperation. Many of them enter in the Dutch service, and make good soldiers. Between Java and Bali are the Straits of Bali.

Lombok is next [to] Bali to the eastward, and about the same magnitude. It produces the same necessaries as Bali but nothing to export.

Sumbawa[2] is next to Lombok to the eastward, an island as big as both the last two mentioned. It produces nothing for export. Between it and Lombok are the Straits of Alas[3], named from a town standing on the shore, about the middle of the straits.

The next islands to the eastward of Sumbawa are the two islands of Sape[4], of small account in commerce, and so is the island of Flores[5], to the eastward of them, though it is

---

[1]   Bali... Lombok. As Hamilton says, he had not visited these places, and could tell little about them. The Dutch had already made contact with Bali in 1597, but made no attempt to conquer the island until 1906. Lombok was a Balinese colony the the seventeenth century. The Dutch took over the island in 1894.

[2]   The island was overtaken by the Makassars from southern Celebes in the seventeenth century and converted to Islam.

[3]   Actually Alas is on the northwest coast of Sumbawa.

[4]   Sape is the easternmost port on Sumbawa. The two islands are Komodo, famous for its dragons, and Rinca.

[5]   The island was under Makassarese and Bugis control before the appearance of the Portuguese, who had established over twenty missions in the east of the island by 1575. Ende, the chief town, was overrun by the Muslims while the priests fled to Larantuka, in the east (not the west, as Hamilton has it).

an island above fifty leagues long, and eighteen broad. In Anno 1703 Captain Wright in the *Leghorn* galley, lost his passage from Banjarmasin on Borneo, to Batavia, and by contrary winds, and strong currents, was driven to this island, and anchored at a town on the west end of it called Larantuka. Finding the place convenient and safe to pass three or four months of the westerly monsoons, he took an house ashore, and kept sometime[s] one part of his ship's crew ashore, and sometimes another, to refresh them. He gave warning to the people of the town not to trust his men, but they, minding their own profit, had trusted the seamen about £100 sterling. A little before he was ready to sail, the creditors came and demanded their money. He refused payment, alleging that a public crier had gone through the town forbidding anybody to trust his men, and that crier was ordered by a magistrate to proclaim the prohibition. The creditors said it was true they could not recover anything by law, but if he valued his own health he would satisfy them, if not in all, yet in part, and so he paid one half, which most of them were content with, but one old witch was not, but threatened his destruction if she had not all her demand paid.

The captain, knowing that the natives were very skilful in the art of poisoning, resolved to prevent their taking any opportunity that way, and so went on board to eat and sleep, and was so cautious that he would not so much as taste their green fruits nor smell their flowers after the time that the old hag threatened him, and yet before he left the place, he found himself much troubled with gripings and fluxes. I was at Batavia when he came there. He could not reach the road with his ship before he anchored, but was forced to anchor without, and sent his boat on board of my ship to desire help to weigh their anchor. I sent a boat with twenty men and an officer to bring their ship into the road, which next morning they did; the poor man was brought to that pass by the effects of poison that he could not walk without being supported, nor could he lift his hand to his head.

I waited on him ashore, and he desired to be carried to his usual quarters, at the sign of the Red Lion, kept by a woman called Black Moll, a native of the island of Flores, and he giving her an account of his condition, and how ignorant he was of the cause of it. She bid him be cheerful, for she knew how he had been poisoned, not by anything taken inwardly, but by a spell, and bid him recollect himself, and try if he could remember if he had not stepped over a bit of paper, or the leaf of a flag, in going in or out of any house, which, after a little pause, he could very well remember he had. She assured him that he should be perfectly well in a month's time, and she performed her promise to admiration. I left Batavia before the cure was perfected, but afterwards when I came to Batavia, she gave me an account that she had restored him to perfect health, and several years after I saw him at Fort St George.

Solor, Lomblen, Pantar, and Alor[1] all lie to the eastward of Flores. They produce a little sandalwood, and cassia-ligna[2]. The Dutch have a factory on Solor.

The island Timor[3] lies within twenty leagues to the south of those four islands above-mentioned. It is a large

---

[1]   These small islands, called Solor, Lodana, Panterra, and Miscomby by Hamilton, lie between Flores and Timor. Western contact was first made by what remained of Magellan's fleet. There was much admixture of the population with Portuguese from Malacca and Macao.

[2]   A kind of cinnamon.

[3]   The Portuguese made contact with the island early in the sixteenth century, and joined in the profitable sandalwood trade. But the Dutch occupied Kupang, the best harbour, from the middle of the seventeenth century; the island was divided between the two colonial powers in the nineteenth century.

island about ninety leagues long, and eighteen broad. The natives acknowledge the King of Portugal their sovereign, and have embraced the Romish religion. They permitted the Portuguese colony of Macao[1] in China to build a fort on it, which they called Lifau[2], and the Dutch a factory called Kupang[3], but would never suffer either to interfere with the government of their country. The Portuguese of Macao drove a very advantageous trade to Timor for many years, and, finding the natives inclined to be passive Catholics, tried by fair means to get the whole government of the country into the church's hands, but could not beguile them that way; therefore they tried force, and commenced a war, but to their cost they found that the Timorese would not lose their liberty for fear of the loss of blood. They chose one Gonsales Gomez their general. He was a native of Timor, and had travelled to Macao and Goa[4]. He allowed the King of Portugal to be the sovereign and protector of their country, and they would be his loyal subjects, providing their laws and liberties might be secured to them.

That war with the city of Macao lasted about fifteen years. It began about the year 1688 and was not quite finished in the 1703, and Macao in the end was ruined by it, for it exhausted both their stock of men and money to such a degree that of 1,000 citizens the town had before the war, there was hardly fifty left at the end of it, and of forty sail of trading ships, not above five left.

[1]   Trade between Timor and Macau was important, but Macau became entangled in the internal revolts of the Timorese between 1664 and 1730 by sending aid to the unpopular governors hailing from Goa in Portuguese India. Macau certainly declined in this period, but not just because of the Timorese involvement.
[2]   The chief town in the former Portuguese Oecussi enclave in the north of west Timor.
[3]   The Dutch settlement on the southwest tip of Timor.
[4]   The Portuguese outpost in India, established 1510.

The viceroy of Goa sent an embassy to Gonsales Gomez in the year 1698 to persuade him to peace, and to accept of a governor-general and an archbishop from Goa, but to no purpose, for they declared that they would admit of no foreign governors in their country, either in church or state.

The product of the island is sandalwood, the best and largest in the world, which is a great commodity in China, also gold and beeswax. The gold is plentiful, but of a low touch, not amounting to twenty carats fine. And all manner of provisions are plentiful and cheap, but there is no anchoring about the island, except at Lifau and Kupang. And the coast is subject to frequent tornadoes, or squalls of wind and rain, introduced with much thunder and lightning.

The natives report that at a certain season of the year, after the southwest monsoons are set in, they can discern an high mountainous land to the southward of them, and continues in sight from December to the latter end of February or the beginning of March, and then disappears. If the report be true, it must be some floating island that comes from and goes to New Holland[1], which is the next tract of land of the south of Timor. These accounts I had from a Portuguese gentleman called Alexander Pinto, who was a captain at Lifau four years, and was bound from Batavia to Goa in Anno 1704. He went passenger with me, and seemed to be a man of probity.

I never met with anybody that could give me any tolerable account of the islands to the eastward of Timor, or of New Guinea, or New Holland and so I'll pass by them, and direct my course to the islands of Banda[2], where cloves,

---

[1]   Australia.

[2]   The history of the original spice islands is long and complex. There was a bitter dispute between the Dutch and the English over their

nutmegs, and mace grow, but are now all engrossed by the Dutch, who allow one of them called Pulau Ai[1] to belong to the English, after they had been at forty years' pains to cut down all the clove and nutmeg trees that grew on it, and have made it death for the natives ever to plant any on it.

The English had also a factory on Pulau Run[2], but were glad to leave it about the year 1618. The Dutch have that island still, with Lontar[3] and Neira[4], where they reap plentiful crops of spice.

I must now steer west-north-west about thirty leagues, to the famous island of Amboina[5], where as real a tragedy

possession; by 1667 the Dutch were in control of them all, and their ruthlessness became proverbial. Most of the original inhabitants were eliminated by Coen in 1621, and certain islands had nutmeg trees uprooted in order to create an efficient monopoly.

[1] Ai is located between the largest island Lonthor and Run to the west.
[2] The English were finally dispossed in 1667 of this westernmost of the Banda Islands.
[3] Great Banda.
[4] Neira possesses the old Portuguese fort now named Nassau and the Dutch fort of Belgica, which dominates the modern town of Bandaneira that remains the centre of the nutmeg trade.
[5] Ambon. 'The story is too well-known to need a place here' was probably true in 1727, and refers to the 'massacre of Ambon'. The Dutch governor-general, Coen, left Ambon in 1622 to return to Batavia, reminding the Dutch governor Herman van Speult to maintain his authority over the English, who were just permitted to trade in the Moluccas. In Ambon they traded under Dutch protection at Fort Victoria. On 23 February 1623 all the members of the English factory (comprising eighteen Englishmen, eleven Japanese and one Portuguese) were arrested by the Dutch and charged with conspiracy to seize the fort. They were tortured, confessed, tried, and beheaded. This event caused a complete breakdown in Anglo-Dutch cooperation; the English withdrew from Batavia, where they had a factory, though this was re-established later. They then transferred to Bantam (see p. 112 note 5), where the sultan willingly protected them, but had to withdraw when the Dutch conquered Bantam in 1682.

was acted on the English as ever happened among friends and allies. The story is too well-known to need a place here. However, at present it has altered its scene, and turned prodigiously religious, having no less than fifty Dutch Protestant churches on that holy island, and the natives are very fond and forward to turn converts, especially since some Amboinese youths have been sent to Holland, and trained up in their universities, and honoured with church orders. They coming back to their own native land loaded with such fine qualifications, and receiving great respect from their masters the Dutch, make the conversion of the populace very easy.

The Dutch have so fortified Amboina, by their own report, that they think it impregnable. It is true Victoria Bay[1] is fathomless till shipping come within a mile of their forts, and there is no other place for anchoring on that side of the island, but I have heard some Dutch officers, in disputing their knowledge of Amboina, say that on that side that fronts the coast of Seram[2], there are several places of anchoring at a mile or two distant from the shore, and never a fort built to impede an enemy's landing, and that if an army superior in force to what the Dutch have at Victoria[3] would march but six or seven leagues by land, they might come on the back of the town and lodge on hills so near it that none could pass the streets in the town, nor appear on their bulwarks or batteries; but this was a secret that the English or French ought not to know.

The island Seram, near Amboina, has also cloves and nutmegs, and the Dutch appropriate that island to

---

[1] Named after Fort Victoria, now Amboina Bay.
[2] The large crescent-shaped island to the north of Ambon.
[3] Now Kota Ambon, the chief town on the island.

themselves, and have a factory on it called Ambay[1]. It is a large island of seventy leagues long, and fifteen broad.

Buru[2] is also a Dutch island producing cloves and nutmegs. It lies west-north-west of Amboina, about thirty-five leagues distant. It is about twenty leagues long, and in the middle ten broad.

Pulau Obi[3] lies in the way between Buru and Gilolo[4], the largest of all the Molucca Islands. The south part of Gilolo is called Batta-China[5], and the equator cuts the island in the middle. On the west side of Gilolo, and at a little distance from it, lie Bacan, Makyan, Motir, Tidore, and Ternate[6]. They are but small islands, but produce the greatest quantities of cloves and nutmegs of all the Molucca islands.

One Captain Ethrington, in a ship called the *Resolution*, made a trip to Gilolo about the year 1692 and got forty tons of spice. He called at Batavia in his way to England, and the Dutch being very solicitous to know where he had been, he freely told them, to let them see the English were not quite ignorant of that navigation, if they had a mind to follow it.

I now continue my course westward along the equator, to the island Celebes[7], the east side of which island, and a great number of smaller ones, are little frequented by

1   Possibly Amahoi, in the southwest.
2   To the west of Ambon.
3   Lying between Seram and Halmahera.
4   Also known as Halmahera, and formerly divided between the sultans of Ternate and Tidore.
5   No longer.
6   Given by Hamilton as Batchian, Matchian, Montil, Tidor, and Ternatey; all islands to the west of Halmahera. Ternate was one of the earliest Portuguese, Dutch and Spanish settlements in the spice islands; a Dutch fort built in 1637 facing the sultan's palace. Tidore, a great rival to Ternate, was likewise an early Islamized sultanate.
7   Sulawesi, the huge orchid-like island in the middle of the Indonesian archipelago.

strangers, but on the southwest corner of it is Makassar[1], where the Dutch have a factory, but its chief product is corn, which indeed all those eastern islands abound in, and consequently in poultry. The natives are of a light olive colour, and the women well-shaped, and pretty beautiful, for which reason they are in great esteem among the Dutch and Chinese, who buy them for bedfellows, and often marry them. The men and women are both short in stature, but well-featured, and well-limbed. They are very loving and faithful if well used, but exceeding revengeful if ill used. The country is populous and very large, being almost 200 leagues long, but the breadth unequal. At the broadest it is about seventy leagues. About thirty leagues westward lies [Borneo].

---

[1]   Now Ujung Pandang; the Makassars had a fiercesome reputation in battle. The Dutch Fort Rotterdam was constructed there after the Treaty of Bungaya in 1667.

Borneo. The village of Long-wei, from Carl Bock, The Head-Hunters of Borneo, 1881.

CHAPTER TEN
[XLV]

BORNEO

Gives an account of Borneo

The great island of Borneo[1] is the largest except California[2] in the known world. The west side of it is for the most part desert. On the south end lies Pulau Laut[3], a most excellent harbour for shipping. The island is but thinly peopled, its product being nothing but rice, but the north end of it lies near many rivers that come out of the pepper countries. The island is about twenty leagues long, but of an unequal breadth, though in some parts it is twelve leagues broad.

There is a channel runs between Pulau Laut and the island of Borneo, about two miles broad, some places narrower, and some broader, and from seven to five fathoms deep, all the way through, and there are several rising grounds along that shore, fit to build houses on, which is a rarity on the sea coasts of Borneo seldom to be

---

[1]   Now known as Kalimantan.
[2]   California, particularly the lower part, was long thought to be an island.
[3]   At the southern end of Borneo, near Banjarmasin.

met with. I heard Mr Sylvanus Landen, who had been chief of Borneo[1], say that he much wondered why the Company of England should have settled a factory at Banjarmasin[2], where they were forced for several years to keep their factory on floats of great trees tied together, and made fast to trees growing in the water on the side of a river with cables made of rattans, and when they built a factory, they were forced first to drive poles in the ground, to make a foundation, as the Dutch do at Amsterdam, and raise earth on them to build upon.

Captain Barré, a very ingenious gentleman, drew the plan, but died[3] before the work was brought to any great forwardness, and Mr Cunningham, who came thither from Pulau Condore[4], when that factory was cut off by their Makassar soldiers[5], came to the head of the Company's affairs. He was bred a surgeon, and had turned virtuoso, would spend whole days in contemplating on the nature, shape, and qualities of a butterfly or a shellfish, and left the management of the Company's business to others as little capable as himself, so everyone but he was master.

Their factory was not half-finished before they began to domineer over the natives who passed in their boats up and down the river, and very imprudently would needs search one of the king's boats, who was carrying a lady of quality down the river, which so provoked the king that he swore revenge, and accordingly gathered an army, and shipped it on large praus, to execute his rage on the factory and shipping that lay on the river. The Company had two

[1]   Landen was president of the EIC factory in Banjarmasin, 1700-2.
[2]   Even today the town, constructed on swamp land, has a large number of houses built on stilts.
[3]   Barré was poisoned by the natives in 1707.
[4]   See Chapter Thirteen, p. 195 note 5.
[5]   In 1705.

ships[1], and there were two others[2] that belonged to private merchants, and I was pretty deeply concerned in one of them[3]. The factory receiving advice of the king's design, and the preparations he had made, left their factory and went on board the shipping, thinking themselves more secure on board than ashore. When all things were in a readiness, the army came in the night[4], with above 100 praus, and no less than 3,000 desperate fellows. Some landed and burnt the factory and fortifications, while others attacked the ships, which were prepared to receive them. The English had made fast nettings from the mizzen[5] to the fore-shrouds[6], about two fathoms high above the gunnel[7], that they might not be too suddenly boarded by the enemy, and to have the opportunity of using their blunderbusses and lances before the enemy could get on their decks. As soon as they in the ships saw the fleet approaching near them, they plied their guns with double round and partridge[8], and made a great carnage, but all did not deter the assailants from boarding, who, when they got as high as the gun-wall or gunnel, were at a loss how to get over the netting, and so were killed with great ease. Some got in at the head door of one of the ships, and killed some English in the forecastle, but they were soon destroyed. The two great ships, though in danger, beat off the enemy with small loss, but the little ships were both burnt, with most of

---

[1] The *Carleton* and the *Blenheim*.
[2] There were three smaller boats, according to Foster, the *Gloucester and Ann*, probably the one in which Hamilton had interests, the *Hawk*, and the *Squirrel*; all three were burnt.
[3] Financially concerned, that is.
[4] Of 25-26 June 1707.
[5] The lowest fore and aft sail.
[6] Ropes forming part of the rigging and supporting a mast.
[7] Gunwale, the upper edge of the side of a ship.
[8] A charge of stones or shots fired together.

their men, and one Dutch gentleman who was obliged to flee from Batavia on one of the small vessels was also burnt in her. His name was Jacob Hoogkamer[1], and had been ambassador to the King of Persia.

I heard some Chinamen say, who were there at the time of the engagement, that the English killed in two hours that the action was hot, above 1,500 men, besides many wounded and maimed, but the English were forced to be gone from their settlement. The king thought his revenge had gone far enough in driving them from their settlement, and finding the loss of the English trade affected his revenue, he let all English who traded to Johor and other circumjacent countries know that he would still continue a free trade with the English on the old footing, but would never suffer them or any other nation to build forts in his country. Several English have been there since, and loaded pepper, and have been civilly treated; and the Dutch sent a ship from Batavia in Anno 1712 to trade with them, but the natives refused commerce with them.

The inland country is very mountainous, but towards the sea very low and marshy, occasioned by the great rains that continue about eight months in the year. It produces rice, and many sort of fruits in great abundance. Pepper is peculiar to the countries about Banjar[2]; and to the westward about Sukadana[3], they have small diamonds, but their waters being inclined to be yellow, are not so much in esteem as those of Golconda[4].

---

[1] The Dutch director in Persia 1698-1791, and ambassador to Shah Husain; Hamilton spells his name Hoogh Camber.
[2] A short form of Banjarmasin.
[3] On the west coast of Borneo.
[4] A city famous for its diamonds, capital of the Shiah kingdom from 1512 to 1687.

The English had formerly a factory at Sukadana, but why they left it I know not, unless it was for the unwholesomeness of the country; yet in Anno 1694 I met with a ship from Fort St George, bound to Sukadana, commanded by one Captain Gullock[1], who had been there the year before, and praised it for a wholesome country, and the inhabitants very civil and obliging. He bought some Surat baftas[2] of me, at 45 per cent on invoice, and expected to make as much himself.

It is reported that on the coast of Borneo between Lava and Sambar[3] there are many cannibals, but I never heard it confirmed by any but Chinese. And from Sambar to Sukadana, the people are civil enough to strangers.

Sambas[4] is the next country of commerce to the northward of Sukadana. It produces but very little pepper, but some gold, pearls, and beeswax, which make it well-frequented by the Chinese, who carry Surat piece-goods[5] from Malacca and Johor, and barter to very good purpose for the aforesaid commodities. Beeswax is the current cash in that country. It is melted but not refined, and cast in moulds of an oblong square, the breadth about two thirds of the length, and the thickness half of the breadth, and a rattan withy[6] to lift them by, cast in the wax. A piece weighs a quarter of a picul, which comes to, in English weight, 34 pound, and a picul[7] is valued in payments at 10

---

[1] Thomas Gullock, commanding the *Success*, was trading from Madras on private account in 1694.

[2] See Chapter Eight, p. 107 note 1.

[3] Both appear on Hamilton's map of Borneo, as Lava and Sobar.

[4] A Malay state on the west side of Borneo, north of Singkawang and Pontianak.

[5] Fabrics woven in standard lengths.

[6] Binder.

[7] One of various units of weight used in China and Southeast Asia, most often the equivalent of 133 pounds. Masscies (maces) is

masscies, or 40 shillings sterling. They have also for smaller payments pieces of eight to a picul and sixteenths, and for smaller money they have cowries. The prince and people are very hospitable and civil, so that strangers trade there with security. I knew a French Armenian[1] who, coming from Manila, had the misfortune to lose his ship on that part of the coast that belongs to the King of Sambas. They had but little goods, for generally Spanish dollars are the common return for goods sold at Manila. When the people that were shipwrecked came ashore, they were carried to the king, who examined what they were, from whence they came, and whither bound, with what they were loaded, and several other interrogatories, and then ordered them provisions, and men and boats to assist them in saving their treasure, for there was but very little lost besides the ship and stores that were not worth the trouble of saving. The king gave him pearls and beeswax for his silver, at such reasonable rates that the Armenian gained 40 per cent at Batavia (whither he went on a China vessel) for the goods he disposed of there. At Batavia he took passage on board a French ship for China, and in their way called at Trengganu[2], when I met with him in 1719. I had the whole account from himself, and saw some beautiful pearls that he was carrying to the China market, and among them a pair of pears[3] worth £50 sterling.

explained by Hamilton himself; the term was previously used in Chapter Six; see p. 88 note 7.

[1] Presumably an Armenian who had taken up residence in France; it would have been interesting to know more about him.

[2] A Malay port and sultanate on the east coast of the peninsula; it is described more fully below.

[3] Pear-shaped pearls.

The Chinese drive a small trade from Siam and Cambodia to the town called Borneo[1] that lies about eighty leagues to the northward of Sambas, and these are all the trading places that lie about the north end of this island that I could hear of. The religion in Borneo is pagan, except in some places on the sea coast there are some Muhammadans. And so I must leave Borneo, and steer my course towards the coast of Johor on the continent, but in my way there are two clusters of islands that lie half-way. One is called Anambas and the other Natuna, but by the natives Siantan[2] is the common appellation for both clusters. Their inhabitants are called Bugis[3], a fierce, desperate people, and the only product of those islands is betel-nut, and the religion Muhammadan. The islands are very high, and may be easily seen in a clear day above fifteen leagues.

[1] Brunei, or rather Bandar Sri Begawan.
[2] Anambas and Natuna are two island groups now belonging to Indonesia; Siantan is one of the larger islands in the Anambas.
[3] Originally from south Celebes, as indicated in p. 119 note 4.

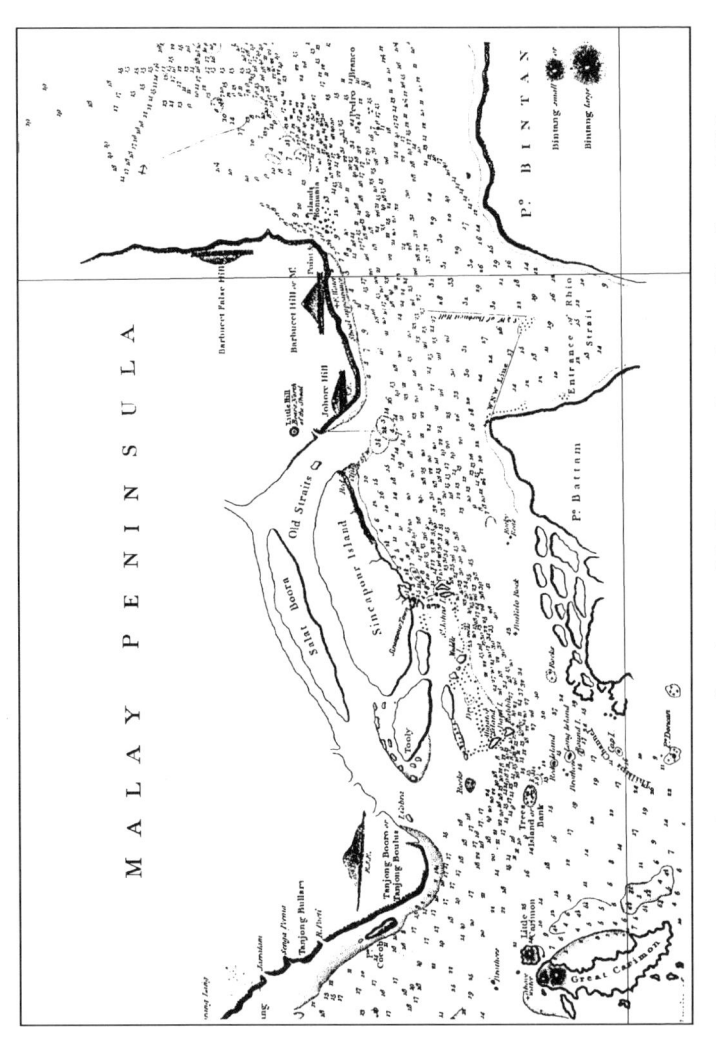

Chart of the Straits of Malacca with Singapore, from James Horsburg, 1823.

FROM JOHOR TO PATTANI

A continuation of the dominions of Johor on the continent, and the islands adjacent

The Johor islands to the north-eastward of the promontory of Romano (from whence I took my departure when I steered among the islands) are first Pulau Tinggi, then Pulau Aor, then Pulau Pisang, and then Pulau Tioman[1], the highest and largest among them. They are all inhabited and produce poultry, and small goats, and some fruits, but no commodities for export. Their religion is Muhammadan.

Pahang[2] lies northwest of Tioman, about twenty leagues distant. Pulau Varela lies in the way, but it is rather a rock than an island, therefore hardly worth noticing. Pahang River has a pretty large island lying in its mouth,

---

[1]   Pulau Tinggi, Aor, Pisang, Tioman: see Chapter Five, p.79 note 2. All located off the southeast coast of the Malay peninsula; Tioman ('Timoun' to Hamilton) was an important watering place as well as a location point on the route to Siam.

[2]   Pahang is a state on the east coast of peninsular Malay; two small islands Pulau Sembilang and Pulau Seri Buat are found on the way from Tioman.

which makes two channels into it. The north entry has no less than four fathoms and an half at high water, and the channel is about an 150 yards broad. Just within the bar is good secure anchoring in six fathoms, and there are good fresh water springs within 200 paces of the seashore. The river is a mile broad, but so full of banks that it is with trouble a small vessel of thirty tons can go to the town, which lies about twelve miles up the river, where I left Rajah Bowncea[1] before I took my ramble among the islands. He was there in Anno 1719 with five or six hundred men to keep that country firm to his father.

Pahang River runs far into the country, and washes the foot of Malacca Hill[2]. There is abundance of gold-dust found in it, and I have seen some lumps of five or six ounces each. They do not dive for the dust above three fathoms, though there are some places in the river above ten deep, and generally where the deepest water is, most gold-dust is found. It has exported some years above eight hundredweight. Along the sides of the river pepper is planted for export, but not above 300 tons in a year, because they want vend[3] for more, though, if they had a market to carry it off, in five years' time they could make a product of 3,000 tons. Besides pepper and gold, there are tin and elephants' teeth, but in no great plenty, and the best canes in the world grow hereabout. The country is woody, and is stored with wild game and fruits, their rivers and sea with great plenty and variety of excellent fish, but the country is not reckoned very healthful, because of the abundance of

---

[1]   See p. 76 note 1 at the end of Chapter Five. This is Hamilton's spelling for what is probably [Indra] Bungsu.

[2]   Mount Ophir. Hamilton has already spoken of this in Chapter Four, p. 61 note 3, and mentioned the quality of Pahang's gold in Chapter Six, p. 88 note 3.

[3]   Lack a market.

rains. Trengganu is the next place of note for commerce, and in Anno 1720 the place of residence of a poor distressd king, who by a senseless devotion to superstition ruined his country and his own family.

I gave an account before[1] of his brother's tragical end, and the daring boldness of a youth that showed him the way to die by his own hand. In 1719 I saw the youth waiting on the king[2], and fanning him with a peacock's tail. In my way to Siam, I called at Trengganu and went to wait on him, and he remembered that he had been acquainted with me five-and-twenty years before. I stayed about a week, and every day he wanted to see me. He often repented his taking the weight of sovereignty on his shoulders, and feared that his end would prove as tragical as his brother's.

Trengganu stands pleasantly near the sea, on the side of a river that has a shallow bar, and many rocks scattered to and again within the river, but room enough in many places to moor small ships very securely to keep them safe from the dangers of the winds or floods. There may be about 1,000 houses in it, not built in regular streets, but scattered in ten or twenty in a place distant a little way from another's villa of the same magnitude. The town is above half-peopled with Chinese, who have a good trade for three of four junks yearly, besides some that trade to Siam, Cambodia, Tonkin and Sambas[3]. When I came back from Siam with my cargo unsold, as I mentioned before, I came to Trengganu to dispose of what I could of my goods,

---

[1] In Chapter Five.

[2] Abdul Jalil. Hamilton was possibly here in 1718, the year in which the sultan was deposed by the ruler of Siak, though Abdul Jalil remained in Trengganu after being overthrown in Johor, before removing to Pahang in 1719.

[3] Sambas is in Kalimantan; see p. 135 note 4.

and to procure a new cargo for Surat; the kind king assisted me in doing both, with all the readiness and cheerfulness imaginable.

While my ship lay in the road, the Bugis came with a fleet of 200 sail of praus, designing to plunder the town of Trengganu; but they were afraid to pass so near our guns as they must have been necessitated to do before they could get into the river. When they came to a place about five leagues off, they sent a prau to my ship, and the officer told me that he had a commission to proffer and pay me 3,000 Spanish dollars if I would let them pass quietly into the river. I ordered him away, and threatened that if they came they should feel the force of my powder and shot. When I came ashore, the king asked me if I would protect him. I told him I would with all the force I had. He wept, as if he had been diffident, and desired that I would take him on board of my ship, and carry him whithersoever I went, for his life was burdensome to him, and he could trust none of his own people. I persuaded him that I was sincere in my resolution to protect him, and that it would look too mean to run away from his kingdom while there was a possibility to regain it.

He told me that he had sent ambassadors to the Dutch at Malacca for assistance, according to the ancient league between his ancestors and them, when they joined their forces to expel the Portuguese from Malacca[1]; but instead of finding relief there, his enemies were assisted with powder and shot, and his rebellious subjects had a safe retreat at Malacca.

I advised him to take protection from the Dutch, and allow them the monopolization of the trade of his country, and to part the revenues between him and them. He

---

[1]   This is true; see p. 57 note 1.

seemed to be offended with the proposal, but said he would be glad if the English would settle in his dominions, and fortify what places they pleased, and that he would willingly come under their protection, and that there were none that ever entertained the Dutch in their countries as guests but would willingly be quit of them again if they could.

There happened to come a French ship thither at that time, being bound to China. The king gave the captain and me an invitation to dinner, and, after we had regaled ourselves, we entered on a discourse of the miserable state of a country under the malignancy of a civil war. He asked us if such calamities had happened to England or France. We assured him there had been often such distempers among us, but that when the disease was cured, our state became as strong and vigorous as ever.

He had several times asked me if I thought the English might be persuaded to settle a colony in his country, so that Pahang might be made a place of great trade, if there were shipping and stock to carry off the pepper and tin which that country alone could produce. I told him I could give him no encouragement to believe they would.

He then despairing of getting an English colony settled, proposed to Mr Pedro-Villamont Garden[1], who commanded the French ship, if he thought the French nation might be induced to settle in his dominions, and the French gentleman gave him hopes that the King of France might be induced to accept of his friendship and settle a colony, providing he would certify his request by a letter, which the King of Johor readily agreed to. It was written in the Malayan language, and translated by a Chinese into

---

[1]   Sic; untraced. Hamilton seems to spell the name of the Frenchman erratically.

Portuguese, and I translated it from that language into English[1]. The original and the English translation were delivered to the French captain, but I never heard of it since[2].

He told me that when I came to Bombay, I should acquaint the governor of the desire he had to live under the protection of the English, and that with 150 men they might bridle the insolence of his own rebellious subjects, and their allies the Bugis too.

Trengganu is a very pleasant and healthful country, and affords a fine landscape from the sea. The hills are low, and covered with evergreen trees that accommodate the inhabitants with variety of delicious fruits, such as lemons, oranges, limes, mangoes, mangosteens, rambutans, lichees and durians; and in the valleys, corn, pulse, and sugar canes. The ground is cultivated by the Chinese, for the lazy Malays cannot take that trouble.

The product of the country is pepper and gold, which are mostly exported by the Chinese. About 300 tons are the common export of pepper, and we have it almost for one half of the price that we pay for Malabar pepper. From the month of October till March, their river is shut up by the bar, which fills up by the impetuosity of the great seas sent on that shore by the northeast monsoons; but in the months of July and August their seas produce the finest fish that ever I saw or tasted. There is one sort exactly like a salmon, both in shape and taste, but the fish is white, as the salmon is red. Their poultry are large, plump and sweet, but beef is scarce, except buffalo beef, and that is plentiful enough.

[1]   Hamilton clearly had a reasonable command of Portuguese.
[2]   After having had their fingers severely burnt in Siam in 1688, the successive French Ministers of the Navy in the Phélypeaux family, the counts of Pontchartrain and Maurepas, were unlikely to welcome any further adventures in the region.

In Anno 1720 the Bugis came to Pulau Kapas[1] which is but five leagues from Trengganu; but there are other islands that lie twelve leagues more southerly, called, in the maps, by the name of Pulau Kapas, but their right name, which the natives call them by, is Pulau Tetang[2].

However, from Pulau Kapas the Bugis sent an embassy to Trengganu pretending an accommodation with the king, to see if he would allow them to enjoy the continent and islands beyond the promontory of Romano, and they would leave him the quiet possession of the rest; and, while they were in a large hall conferring, some unusual sudden noise happened to be heard from without, which the guilty Bugis taking to be some design in execution against them, one of them runs to the king, and krissed[3] him to the heart, which made a very great disorder, and many were killed on both sides; and what Bugis remained got on board of their galleys, and posted to their fleet at Pulau Kapas with the news of what had happened at Trengganu, and next day the Bugis went into the river and plundered the town, except certain houses which belonged to the Datobandar[4], or first minister, whom the king in his lifetime ever mistrusted, but by the ill situation of his affairs was obliged to hide his thoughts and defer his resentments till a proper time.

The next place to the northward in the Johor territories is Pattani[5]. It was formerly the greatest port for trade in all

---

1 A short distance from the shore and the small port of Marang.
2 Pulau Braba.
3 They ran him through with a kris. Whether this episode in fact relates to Abdul Jalil in Trengganu is in doubt.
4 Datobandar. A contracted form of Dato (a Malay title of dignity) and shahbandar, harbour master.
5 Hamilton makes no mention of the matrilineal queens of Pattani nor of it paying somewhat spasmodic allegiance to Siam. Pattani's great

those seas, but the inhabitants being too potent to be afraid of the king's laws, they became so insolent that merchants were obliged to remove their commerce to countries of more security. It was the staple port for Surat shipping, and from Goa, Malabar and Cormandel they had a good trade, and so they had from China, Tonkin, Cambodia and Siam; but the merchants, finding no restraint on robbers and murderers, were obliged to give their trade a turn into another channel, which was a great advantage to Batavia, Siam[1] and Malacca, where they were kindly used, and in those ports it has continued ever since.

The Johor dominions reach but four or five leagues farther north, which, like most borderers are inclined to rapine, and lying so near another's dominions where they may be screened from the power of their own laws when they commit depredations, it makes them exercise their villanies with impunity. Between Trengganu and Pattani lie the islands of Redang[2]. They are uninhabited, but sometimes the saleiters or Malay freebooters frequent them, and when they meet with trading vessels that they are able to master, they make prize of them, and carry the men into other countries than where they belong to, and sell them for slaves; and when they meet with no purchase at sea, they go ashore in the nights, and steal all they can get. Men, women and children go all into the booty; but the China vessels afford them most prizes.

period of prosperity was the sixteenth and early seventeenth century.
2   Siam here means the capital, Ayutthaya.
3   Redang, along with Perhentian Kecil and Besar, Ru, Lang Tengah, and Bidung Laut.

The kings of Johor ever paid homage to the kings of Siam by sending them a rose made of gold in a golden box once in three years[1]. The year 1719 happened to be the year that the rose came, for I saw the messenger that brought it at Siam, where he had orders from his master to know how my affairs went, with a proffer of the king's service if I came back into his country.

---

[1]   Hamilton is here describing the *bunga mas*, the golden flowers of obeisance.

View of the river Meinam, with houses built on poles of Bambous, from E. Kaempfer, Description of the Kingdom of Siam 1690.

SIAM: ITS CAPITAL, JUSTICE, CUSTOMS, AND RECENT REVOLUTION

G ives an account of the dominions and city of Siam, with remarks on the revolution that happened there

Singora[1] is the first town on the king of Siam's dominions. On that side it is under the goverment of Ligor, which was once the metropolis of a kingdom of the same name, but, by civil dissensions, it became a prey to the King of Siam.

Singora stands on the side of a large river. It yields some tin, elephants' teeth, agala-wood and coarse gold, but the inhabitants meet with so great discouragements in digging for tin that there is very little to be procured: and what is manufactured is bought up by the Dutch factory at Ligor.

Ligor[2] lies about twelve leagues to the northward of Singora, and between them lies a low uninhabited island,

---

[1]   Songkhla, which was periodically at war with Pattani and in revolt against Ayutthaya; it was offered to the French in 1685, who turned it down.

[2]   See Chapter One, p. 16 note 2. Nakhon Si Thammarat also revolted against Ayutthaya in the seventeenth century; King Prasat Thong sent the Japanese Yamada Nagamasa to quell the revolt of 1629.

called Papier[1]. It reaches from Singora within three leagues of Ligor River. It is well stored with wild buffaloes, hog and deer, which are free for all persons to kill at pleasure. The road of Ligor lies two leagues from the river, and about a league within the river's mouth stands the Dutch factory, a pretty commodious house, built of brick after the Dutch fashion. The town stands about two miles above the factory. It is built of bamboos, and thatched with reed. There are many pagan temples[2] in it, which have steeples built very high, in the form of very sharp pyramids. They are so small that in the road they look like ships' masts. It produces abundance of tin, but the Dutch engross[3] it all.

Pulau Cara[4], a high island, lies about twelve leagues off Ligor. The next place of note is Cui[5], a place that produces great quantities of tin and elephants' teeth, but all are sent to the city of Siam or Odia[6] for the king's use. The rest of the coast being little frequented, I will pass by it, and steer for the bar of Siam.

The city stands on an island in the River Menam, which by turnings and windings makes the distance from the bar about fifty leagues. The country is low, and as fruitful as

---

[1]   Perhaps the peninsula of Pakpranang; Foster thinks it is Ko Yai.
[2]   Nakhon Si Thammarat is famous for its numerous Buddhist temples; the town is often called *muang phra*, city of priests.
[3]   Monopolize.
[4]   Ko Kra, a small uninhabited island some 100 km east of Songkhla. On Hamilton's map he shows, from north to south, south of Cui and north of Papier, Bardea, Sancroy, and Cornio. These were often known to seventeenth century travellers as Bardi, Cori or Sancori, and Cornon, the Malay names for the modern Thai forms of Ko Tao, Ko Pangan, and Ko Samui respectively.
[5]   Kuiburi, not Chaiya, as Foster hypothesizes. It was an important point on the overland route between Ayutthaya and Mergui.
[6]   Ayutthaya, the old capital, destroyed in 1767, standing on the Menam (i.e. river) Chao Phya, already mentioned in p.13 note 1.

any spot of ground in the world, in rice, legumen, fruits and roots, cattle wild and tame. And the river abounds in many species of excellent fish, which plentifully indulge the inhabitants, and make them indolent and lazy, and consequently proud, superstitious and wanton.

The city is reckoned ten miles round the walls, and many canals from the river pierce through the city from all quarters. The walls of the city are high and thick, built of stone and brick; but the houses of the natives, though large, are low, built on stakes driven into the ground, about ten or twelve foot high; but the Muhammadans, Chinese and Christians raise the grounds they build on high enough to be secure from the yearly inundations. The natives' houses are raised on those stakes on the same account, and as their walls are built of bamboo and reeds, their roofs are built of the same materials, and are all thatched, except what are built on terra firma, and they are generally tiled. There are many arched bridges in the city, built of brick or stone, and some of wood. The floors of the natives' houses are made of split bamboo or reeds made fast together, so that one cannot move on them without both noise, and shaking them.

The three palaces of their kings[1] and some temples are the only magnificent edifices in the city; and some steeples belonging to the temples are gilded with gold on the outside, and in a sunshine they reflect the rays so strongly that at two or three miles' distance they disturb the eye when looked upon.

They have many large temples well-decorated after their way, and well-stocked with gilded images of gods and goddesses, of the priests' contrivance and canonizing, and

---

[1]   The Front Palace (Wang Na), the Royal Palace (Wang Luang), and the Rear Palace (Wang Lang).

they never want devotees to adore them, who pay their deceitful imposers very well for deceiving them; but they are not the only people that are so cunningly deluded, for the fatal custom has spread universally in all the corners of the world.

The great God who created the universe they have no image of, nor can they make any of him, because he never showed himself in any bodily shape, and therefore they can form no idea of his shape, dimensions or beauty; but Tipedah[1], the great God's partner, has often showed himself, and him they worship in his image with the highest adoration. Phra Prom and Sommo Cuddem [Samana Gautama] his friends they adore with the second degree in worship; and Prapout and Samsay[2] have the third sort of veneration paid to their images.

They have many little deities inferior to those above-mentioned whom they adore as patrons or protectors of several tribes of men, and other animals of different countries and cities, of health, prosperity and other chances and casualties, so everyone is at liberty to choose his own patron or protector, and worship him according to his own mind, but none are persecuted for the opinion of the way he is to worship, either the great or the little gods[3]. That heavenly frenzy is only a raging mad distemper that affects the melancholic brains of the Western world.

I was in one temple, pretty large, built exactly four-square, and each square contained just an hundred images. They were placed in notches[4] or domes about four foot

[1] Probably *tevada*, heavenly being.
[2] Sommo Cuddem, Phra Prom, Prapout and Samsay: see Chapter One, p. 11, note 4. Phra Phrom is holy Brahma. Samsay is probably used here to indicate an image.
[3] Hamilton's conception of Buddhism was, to say the least, confused.
[4] Apparently a variant of niches.

from the ground. There were more goddesses than gods[1], and all were in a sitting posture cross-legged, as tailors sit on their shopboards. Their noses were low and small, their visage long, their ears large, and the lappets[2] of them thick and plump. They sat promiscuously in those notches, and all clothed in one livery of gold leaf. They were almost as big as full-grown men and women, but very different in their substances. The priests told us that some were of pure gold, others of tical silver[3], which has no alloy in it, some of copper, and some of brass, and some of baked clay; but, for want of sumptuary laws among them, it was hard to know the gentleman from the beggar by their garb, or a lady from a laundress.

In one temple, as I was informed, stands the famous Samsay twenty yards in height. He is in a right lineal descent from little Samsay who caused so much war between Siam and Pegu, which never ended but with the dissolution of the Pegu empire. In most of their temples there are frightful dragons standing sentinels at their gates[4], but whether they are placed there to keep in the gods, or to keep out devils, I know not.

There are reckoned no less than 50,000 clergymen or tallapois belonging to the temples in and about the city of Siam; but they are easy to the state, having no stated benefices or other revenues, and yet they are plentifully supplied with all the necessaries of life by the charity and benevolence of the laity.

---

[1] They were all male, images of the Buddha, whose asexuality is emphasized in the iconography, which obviously confused Hamilton.

[2] Lobes, as in p. 31 note 4.

[3] Silver pure enough to be used for coin, 0.900 fine.

[4] The guardian giants or *yaksa*.

There is one temple about three miles below the city, on the opposite side of the river, called the Fishes Temple[1], because annually in the month of September, when the floods overflow the low ground (as in Egypt) there are good numbers of fishes almost like small salmon that frequent a pond close to that temple, and are to be found in no other place in the Siam dominions, and they are so tame that they will come close to our boats, and frisk and play on the surface of the water if anybody has a mind to feed them with bread, coconut meat, or other food that does not easily separate. 'Tis only to hold some near the surface of the water, and they will take it familiarly from the hand. I have often taken pleasure to feed them and see them play, but as soon as we leave off feeding them, they will withdraw, so that hardly one is to be seen till a new supply of victuals is offered to them.

But none dares offer to take one of them for fear of raising a zealous sanctified mob, who punish small faults with the greatest severities, and those fishes, being consecrated to the god of that temple, are securely protected by the consecration. They continue about the temple till the middle of December, that the floods begin to draw off the ground, and then they depart, and are seen nowhere in any river or pond belonging to Siam till September brings them back to their temple.

Whatever animal comes within the verge of a temple, it is secured from pursuit or violence. I knew a Portuguese inhabitant of Siam who shot a crow as it sat on the branch of a tree that grew near a temple, on which the priests raised a mob who broke both the poor man's legs and arms, and left him in the field for dead, but some Christians coming accidentally by carried him in a boat, in that

---

[1]   Probably the island temple at Bang Pa-in, with a royal palace marked in La Loubère's map.

deplorable state, to a French surgeon[1], who set his bones and cured him. I saw him alive and well in Anno 1720[2].

The French have a bishop at Siam, with a church and a seminary for the education of converts. They stand a little above the city, on the opposite side of the river[3]. They make but few converts, except when corn is dear, and then some of the poorer sort receive baptism, which entitles them to a maintenance from the church, but when plenty returns, they throw away their beads and brazen saint[s], and bid farewell to Christianity. In Anno 1720 there were not above seventy Christians in and about Siam, and they the most dissolute, lazy, thievish rascals that were to be found in the country.

The bishop was one Mr de Cisée[4] a man of about eighty years of age, who, in a famine that happened there in Anno 1708 took up about £3,000 sterling from the king to buy corn for the support of his church and such poor Siamese as were converted by the necessity of the times, who relapsed again as soon as the famine ceased, and the poor old bishop cannot leave the country till that debt be discharged. He is superstitiously zealous for his religion, and would fain go to Cochin-China or Tonkin to die a martyr, because it is death by their law to preach any foreign doctrine without leave first obtained from their kings[5].

---

[1] Probably a Missionary doctor.
[2] Hamilton was in Ayutthaya in 1718; the wrong date is repeated below.
[3] The seminary was for long located at Mahapram, on the west bank.
[4] The French bishop Louis Champion de Cisé, born 24 September 1648, was in fact 70 in 1718, and his church was dedicated to St Joseph. The Christians were descendants of Portuguese, Cochin-Chinese and Tonkinese, with a very few Siamese and Peguan converts. The mission was always very poor.
[5] Both Tonkin and Cochin-China (and China too) objected to Christianity, since it denied the link between the rulers and heaven.

Whatever principles he may have had in religion I know not, but I am sure that he was a diminutive moralist, which I knew by experience in seducing some of my seamen, who were black Christians, to leave my ship at Siam, contrary to his promise, which obliged me to buy slaves to supply their places; but I left him some cause to repent of his folly and breach of promise.

There were four or five priests there besides the bishop, one whereof always attends the college, and the others officiate daily in the church. They live abstemiously, but, I believe, rather through force than choice, for their incomes are very small, as charity and piety are very cold among their flock. The Portuguese have also a church there[1], built on the side of the river opposite to the lower end of the town; but their priests are generally so scandalous in their lives that few frequent their church or care for their conversation. The Chinese, being very numerous in Siam, have several small temples, but none remarkable for their structure or beauty.

The Dutch have a factory there, about a mile below the town, on the same side of the river. Their greatest investments are in tin, sappanwood and deers' skins, which they buy up for the Japan market. The Siam market takes off but little European goods; however the Dutch chief makes a pretty good figure there.

The English for many years had also a factory there[2], till about the year 1686 the East India Company seeking

[1] São Domingo.

[2] This was never a commercial success, thanks largely to the private trade and outright duplicity of the Company's servants. The factory was first established in 1612 and was closed in 1622. It was reopened about 1659, closed again, reopened in 1674 and burnt down in 1682 as a result of a quarrel between Burnaby and Potts, respectively a supporter and an enemy of the Levantine chief minister and former company employee, Phaulkon.

occasions to pick a quarrel with the Siamese, in order to withdraw, they took hold of such as they could first find, though never so frivolous. The first was about Anno 1684. The *Carolina*, bound from England to China, had the misfortune to lose her passage, and coming to Siam to pass away the northeast monsoons, and the King of Siam[1] having occasion for some stores for shipping out of the *Carolina*'s cargo, to equip ships that he had built in order to humble the Cambodians and the Cochin-Chinese, who disturbed the navigation of his country, he civilly requested the English chief to supply him at the prices the same commodities used to be sold at to merchants, but he could not find that favour, which he resented, and threatened to disturb their commerce[2]. At length they supplied him with some part of what he demanded, to avert the ill consequences that might happen by a total refusal. This was represented to the Company in the darkest colours, and they thought that sufficient to ground a war on; but they had, at that time, a fleet of large ships which they had equipped to regain their trade of Bantam and other places, which the Dutch had insolently robbed them of; but they were disappointed by the deep politics of King Charles II as is before observed[3].

---

[1] King Narai, d. 1688.

[2] The ship in fact was probably the *Delight*, two of whose officers were imprisoned in 1684 for refusing the sell the king nails from the ship's stores.

[3] Charles II (r.1660-1685) secretly promised to join France in a war against the Netherlands. The Dutch War of 1672-4 was unpopular and unsuccessful. From 1670 Charles received a secret subsidy from Louis XIV and promised to declare himself a Catholic; his moves were blocked by Parliament, fearing a Popish plot. It was perhaps fear of irritating Parliament further that prevented more attacks on the Dutch.

However, the King of Siam continued his indulgence to the Company and their servants, in much affluence and luxury, continually carousing in debaucheries with wine and women, till their common salaries and gains by trade were in no proportion to their extravagant expenses. However that being a free country, they had liberty to spend their own and their masters' estates as they pleased.

The King of Siam having formed the design of a war, as above-mentioned, with Cambodia and Cochin-China,[1] employed a good number of English who had resorted to Siam to partake of the king's indulgence and bounty, and to help the Company's servants to spend their money. All the English who had a mind to list themselves on board of his fleet had great encouragement of honourable posts and good salaries well paid, and they did perform actions in the war worthy of the bravery and courage of the English nation, by which the king's favour to the English increased more than before the war[2].

One Mr Potts[3] happened to be chief of the English factory at that time, who by his extravagant luxury had

---

[1]   A revolt occurred in 1682 in Cambodia against King Chey Chettha IV, fomented by his cousin Ang Non, who was supported by the King of Cochin-China Hien-vong. Chey Chetha managed to suppress the revolt with Siamese help. Ang Non began agitating again in 1684, and Chey Chettha again sought King Narai's help. But Siamese troops sent to help the Cambodian king were beaten in 1685.

[2]   Hamilton's source of information was probably Phaulkon's English secretary Bashpool (p. 166 note 3), who may well have been flying the flag here.

[3]   Samuel Potts arrived in Ayutthaya in 1674 as scrivener, together with two young assistants. He complained of "several great enormities" in the Company's business, and Richard Burnaby was sent from Bantam to investigate. Burnaby soon struck a friendship with George White, a pilot working for the Siamese, and his brother Samuel, and both joined the EIC. Burnaby befriended the young

rioted away a great part of his masters' goods and money, and had run his own credit out of doors. He then began to form projects how to clear accounts with his masters and creditors without putting anything in their pockets. The first was on 500 chests of Japan copper, which his masters had in specie at Siam, and they were brought into account of profit and loss, for so much eaten up by the white ants, which are really insects, that by a cold corroding liquid quality can do much mischief to cloth, timber, or on any other soft body that their fluids can penetrate, but copper is thought too hard a morsel for them. However, I saw that article in the Company's accounts, as they were remitted from Siam to Bombay, and were in Mr Vaux's custody at Surat afterwards.

But that small article of 2,500 pounds went but a small way towards clearing of his accounts. So after supper one night as they were merrily carousing, the factory was set on fire, and that balanced all other accounts. Mr Potts alleged to the king that his subjects the Siamese had done that mischief, and expected the king to be accountable for losses and damages sustained by the Company and their servants.

The king, on the other hand, proffered to prove that Mr Potts and his drunken companions had done it, and that he expected the Company should be accountable to his subjects for the loss they had sustained by the fire, which

Levantine of obscure origin, Phaulkon, who was brought to Siam from Bantam in his ship. Potts, a protégé of Lord Berkeley, naturally jealous of the favour shown to Phaulkon, a former cabin-boy from Cephalonia, complained about both Burnaby and Phaulkon. Potts was then in dispute with Phaulkon over debts, was told to wind up the Company's affairs, and then was accused of arson when the Company's factory burnt down (see p. 156 note 2). He finally left Ayutthaya in January 1684. Relations between Phaukon and the Company continued to deteriorate (see the section on Mergui, Chapter Three, p. 42 note 2).

had burnt several houses that lay near the factory. However, the Company adhered to the just complaints of their honest servants, and thought that the king's refusal to make good their demands was a sufficient piece of ground to build their war on. However, the Company, considering that a war could bring them no advantage, thought it enough to bully the Siamese, but never declared a war.

In the year 1685[1] the Company sent two ships to the Bar of Siam. One was the *Herbert* of 800 tons, the other the *Prudent Mary* of 400 to frighten the Siamese, but they did no damage to them, and the Siamese treated them civilly[2].

About 1680 there was one Constantine Phaulkon[3], a Greek by birth, that some years before had shipped himself steward of an English ship at London, bound to India, and being ordered for Siam, and finding some ill-treatment on board, he deserted from the ship, and fled to a small village some distance from the city, where he amused himself in learning the Siam language. He being a sober, ingenious, and industrious person, soon made himself master of the language, and served as an interpreter for the English at court, where he was remarkably taken notice of, and got a

---

[1]   It was 1686, as Forbin's account shows (see note 2 below). The *Herbert* was captained by Henry Udall and came from England.

[2]   Far from it, as Forbin's account of his boarding the *Prudent Mary* and seizure of Captain Lake (on Phaulkon's orders) makes clear (see *Memoirs of the Count de Forbin*, London, 1731, I, pp.184-194). Lake was said by Forbin to be finally released after settling "his Affair for Ten thousand Crowns, which M. Constance thought fit to put in his Pocket." Collis maintains Lake died in prison in Ayutthaya.

[3]   See p. 158 note 3. Phaulkon, a highly controversial person, rose through a combination of intelligence, luck, flattery and patronage to the position of chief minister under King Narai. He amassed a fortune, most of which he lost, along with his life, in the revolution of 1688. Hamilton's account of Phaulkon's life is generous and untrue in some details.

post there. His behaviour recommended him to greater preferments, so that in a very few years he became prime minister of state, and behaved himself so well in that high station that everything belonging to the state of the country prospered, so that Siam became the richest and power-fullest kingdom in that part of the world[1].

The Jesuits hearing that one of the Romish commu-nion[2] sat at the helm of the Siam affairs, and it being a rich country, brought whole troops of them into Siam, who got the whole management of affairs into their hands, through the interest of the Barkalon[3], that being the appellation of first minister. They tickled themselves with the fancy of bringing the whole kingdom of Siam under the Pope's jurisdiction, and in Anno 1683 the first year of his ministry[4], they got the king to send an embassy to the King of France[5], which ambassador came also to London, and settled a treaty of commerce for the English that should trade in Siam.

[1] Siam's prosperity can hardly be exclusively attributed to the few years Phaulkon was in power, as Hamilton implies.

[2] Phaulkon converted (from Anglicanism, acquired while working for the EIC, and to which he may have converted earlier from Orthodoxy) under Jesuit influence in 1682 just prior to his marriage. The Jesuit presence only increased significantly in 1687 when Tachard from France returned with several companions with the La Loubère-Céberet embassy.

[3] A Portuguese corruption of Phra Klang, the minister in charge of trade and therefore foreigners; not the chief minister, as is often held.

[4] The date 1683 is probably correct, though it is disputed.

[5] The first embassy to France left before Phaulkon's rise to power, in 1681; it never arrived, being shipwrecked off Madagascar. The second mission left in 1684 to find out what happened to the first, and went via London; Evelyn's diary entry for September 1684 records the event. The mission met Charles II in September but no treaty was settled.

The Jesuits imposed on the King of France[1], and made him believe that if he would send an embassy to Siam, that king would leave his own superstition, and embrace theirs. Accordingly an ambassador was sent[2], with many valuable French curiosities, and among them a very fine mass-book, with beautiful cuts[3] of all the first-rate saints in the Romish calendar[4].

On the ambassador's arrival, he was received with the respect due to his character, and when the presents were laid before the king, according to custom, he seemed much pleased with their curiosity, but when he viewed the pictures in the mass-book, he asked a Jesuit who was interpreter[5] what they were, who answered that they were the pictures of holy men now in heaven, and such as his brother the King of France adored, and, as he designed an eternal friendhip with His Majesty, he hoped that he would also adore those pictures, and worship the images of those saints, rather than those idols that were worshipped all over his dominions. The king returned answer that the gods of his country had been auspicious to them who lived in it

---

[1]   Hamilton is roughly correct in his summary. Vachet, the 1684 mission's interpreter, persuaded Louis XIV's confessor, the powerful Jesuit Father de la Chaise, that a sufficiently grand embassy could probably persuade King Narai to convert to Catholicism. King Narai of course had no such intention, and no one would have dared suggest it to him.

[2]   The Chevalier de Chaumont, in 1685, seconded by the Abbé de Choisy as co-adjutant ambassador; both left accounts of their stay.

[3]   Engravings.

[4]   Hamilton's anti-clericalism shows through; the presents were numerous and exceedingly grand, and comprised far more valuable items than those listed here.

[5]   The Jesuits had few with a sufficient command of Siamese; it was more likely one of the French Missionaries, either the Bishop of Metellopolis, Louis Laneau, Father Bénigne Vachet or the Abbé de Lionne.

for time out of mind, and as it would be unjust and ungrateful to banish those gods that had been so long very kind to his predecessors and himself, so he could not turn his old gods off and take new ones in their places that he did not so well know, and that he would oblige his brother of France in anything but that.

The King of France complimented Mr Phaulkon with the order of knighthood[1], and in his letter to him, wherein he recommended the French affairs to his care, particularly that of religion, he styled him loving cousin and counseller.

After the embassy was gone from Siam to France, the Jesuits thought of nothing but bringing the trade of Siam under the power of the French, and in order to do that, got the king to order the building of a fort[2] on the river's side, opposite to the fort of Bangkok, a town about twenty leagues below the city of Siam, and to have it manned with a garrison of French to be paid by the exchequer of Siam, and all this was granted according to their mind.

The fort is a regular tetragon, and can mount about eighty great guns. When the French got possession they grew intolerably arrogant, which made the Siamese uneasy, and murmured at the king's weakness, but that was in

---

[1] This confuses the sequence of events. It was not the first French embassy of 1685 which presented Phaulkon with the title of count and made him a knight of the order of St Michael, but the second, led by Simon de La Loubère seconded by Claude Céberet du Boullay, in 1687. The investiture took place on 23 November, when La Loubère handed over the title deeds for land carrying the title of count of France and permitting Phaulkon to bear three fleur-de-lys in his arms. This second embassy had the character more of a military expedition, and instructions to seize Bangkok, seen as 'the key to the kingdom', if it were not handed over voluntarily.

[2] The fort on the left bank was already begun, and the Chevalier de Forbin spent much time in 1686 improving it. The 'fort of Bangkok' was older, on the Thonburi or right bank.

private, for certain destruction is the sure reward of talking publicly of any mismanagement of the state, for a king of Siam can no more err in politics than a pope can in matters of faith.

Yet about the year 1688[1], by some malevolent planet that overruled his actions, he made a war with his neighbours the kings of Cambodia, and Cochin-China[2]. He sent an army by land and a fleet by sea to carry on the war, but was not successful by land. However, in the land army there was a mean person[3], a citizen of Siam, who kept a fruit-shop; he had a bold, daring spirit, and behaved himself so well on all occasions in the land war that he

[1]   The date is correct; the coup d'état of Petratcha took place in Lopburi on 18 May.

[2]   In 1688 there was another revolt in Cambodia, the origin being a dispute between the Chinese there, in which Ang Non, the Cochin-Chinese protégé, lent his assistance. It was defeated and tribute to Cochin-China was refused. Cochin-China invaded and Ang Non once more tried to seize the throne. The Cambodian king Chey Chettha IV eventually agreed to joint Siamese-Vietnamese suzerainty. This represented something of a defeat for Siamese diplomacy.

[3]   Hamilton is singularly ill-informed about the origins of Petratcha (the grandfather of the king reigning at the time of his visit). He was a son of Narai's wetnurse, who was given the Palace of the Rear as residence and given the important post of chief of the royal elephant stables and their numerous personnel. He plotted against the king's two half-brothers and conspired against Narai, whose health was declining, finally imprisoning him in his palace on 18 May 1688 and arresting Phaulkon. Narai died naturally, on 10 or 11 July, though his end was probably hastened by his invidious position. Petratcha killed Narai's protégé, Mom Pi, and then the king's two half-brothers by placing them in a sack and beating them to death with sandlewood clubs. Petratcha is not known to have led Siamese troops to Cambodia or Cochin-China. The source of Hamilton's information was, as is made clear in the text, Phaulkon's secretary Bashpool, who, having spent some time in prison as a result of Petratcha's coup, was not likely to speak favourably of him.

came to preferment, and at last was made generalissimo, and then ended the war to the satisfaction of the whole army abroad, and his prince at home. But when he brought back the army to Siam, seeing the king wrapped up in the opinion he had of the Jesuits' counsels, and the management they had in the affairs of state by the countenance of the king and his first minister my lord Phaulkon, he picked a quarrel with the king, and having most of the army at his devotion, seized his master and put him to death, after the manner of royal criminals, or as princes of the blood are treated when convicted of capital crimes, which is by putting them into a large iron cauldron, and pounding them to pieces with wooden pestles, because none of their royal blood must be spilt on the ground, it being, by their religion, thought great impiety to contaminate the divine blood by mixing it with earth. And after he had murdered his master, he summoned all the mandarins in the city to hold a council in the palace.

My lord Phaulkon, for that was generally his designation, had, by his civil deportment towards people of all ranks and degrees, so ingratiated himself that he had a stronger party by far, both in city and country, than the general[1], and besides, had all the fleet[2] at his devotion. Many of my lord's friends dissuaded him from obeying the summons, but to raise the forces of the city, and revenge the death of the king[3], and many officers of the army that detested the regicide would have come over to his party,

---

[1]   Phaulkon did not have the upper hand, and may well have been in some disfavour in the early part of 1688. He did indeed hurry to the palace in Lopburi on 18 May 1688, where he was seized by Petratcha's men, imprisoned, tortured, and finally put to death on 5 June in Thalé Chupson outside Lopburi.

[2]   Siam's fleet, mostly of merchant ships, was not notably significant.

[3]   The king was not yet dead.

which at least was above 50,000 strong, but being infatuate, he was deaf to all good advice, and went to the palace, where as soon as he had set his foot, he was seized by the general's guards, and beheaded, so the usurper took the sovereignty into his own hands, and at that instant was by *jure divino* made an infallible favourite of heaven, and the sun, moon, and stars had the honour to be his near relations.

Had my lord Phaulkon followed his friends' advice, or had courage answerable to his other good qualities, he had certainly been honoured with the diadem in Siam[1], and if he had introduced popery in the place of paganism, he had been honoured with a place in the Pope's almanac, but his pusillanimity[2] made him unworthy of both.

I had this account from my lord's secretary Mr Bashpool[3], who, on his master's death, was clapped up in prison, and lay three years with his neck in the cangue[4], which are a pair of stocks made of bamboos, and was never taken out but in order to be severely whipped, to make him accuse rich men whom the usurper had a mind to destroy, that he might seize their estates under the umbrage of justice and law.

---

[1]   Phaulkon's enemies – and he had many – accused him of wanting to become king himself. He was, however, no fool, and must have foreseen the impossibility of this: the entire country would have opposed him. He is much more likely to have plotted to rule through a pliant Siamese, either Mom Pi, the king's favourite, or possibly through Princess Yothathep, the king's only child.

[2]   Phaulkon had many faults, but pusillanimity was not one of them.

[3]   Joseph Bashpool; little is known about him other than that he was Phaulkon's English secretary. He may have been another former EIC employee, like his master.

[4]   It was placed around the neck, not the feet, so was not quite the same as being in the stocks.

I saw my lady Phaulkon in Anno 1719[1] and she was then honoured with the superintendency of His Majesty's confectionery. She was born in Siam of honourable parents[2], and at that time much respected both in the court and city for her prudence and humanity to natives and strangers when they came into difficulties or under the weight of oppressions from the officers of the court or city.

When the Siam ambassador returned from France and England[3], in the murdered king's time, his master, among many other questions, asked him if the King of France had

[1]   Actually 1718.
[2]   The origins of Madame Constance, as she was known to the French party, are much discussed. Her proper name was Maria Guyomar de Pinha, and she was also known as Dame Marie Guimard. She was part-Portuguese, part-Japanese, and her parents were known as Master Phanick, a half-Bengali half- Japanese, and Ursula Yamada. Her mother may have been less virtuous than appeared, for she was reputed to have given birth to children of various colours, one being quite pale and fathered by a Jesuit priest. As noted above, Phaulkon, after renouncing Protestantism, and becoming a Catholic in May 1682, then married Maria Guyomar. She had a considerable reputation for her charity, piety and good works. She was arrested after the May 1688 coup, managed to escape by bribing her jailors, and sought protection of the French at their fort in Bangkok on 4 October (her late husband was after all a recently ennobled peer of France). But the French general, Desfarges, handed her back to the Siamese, notwithstanding the views of his scandalized officers. She was condemned to perpetual slavery, which lasted until the death of the usurper Petratcha in 1703. Father Maldonado wrote that she, her mother, aunts and grandmother were cast into the kitchens of the princess Yothathep (Narai's only child, who was forced to marry Petratcha after the death of her father). Maria Guyomar managed to resist the advances of Petratcha's son and successor Sorasak (Sua, r. 1703-1709) and seems by the time of Hamilton's visit to have re-established a position in society.
[3]   Kosa Pan, the chief Siamese ambassador to Louis XIV in 1686, and his party never set foot in England. They landed at and departed from Brest on French ships.

any palaces like his at Siam for beauty and magnitude, and the poor man unadvisedly told him truth, that in France were many finer, nay, that the King of France's horse stables in Paris exceeded any buildings in India, which His Majesty took so ill that he disgraced him[1], and was very near losing his head for his telling truth.

The King of Siam is as fond of lofty titles as the King of Pegu. Besides his proximity with the heavenly luminaries, he is a god on earth, in whose court are to be found justice, mercy, and benevolence to mankind, with such a train of senseless hyperboles and at last, to illustrate all the rest, he is king of the white elephant, a title that none disputes with him but the King of Pegu.

The king bestows his anniversary blessing on his people in the month of September, when he passes through the city attended with a numerous train of elephants, among whom is the white elephant, but he is only of a cream colour, and I have seen several at Bangri[2], a village near Junk Ceylon, as white as him. All the elephants that day are dressed in their finest trappings, with drums, trumpets, hautboys, and other musical instruments making a noise as they go along, but whether it is to divert His Majesty or his elephants I know not, but I am sure the noise was harsh in my ears.

While he is making his elephantine cavalcade through the city, the populace dares not look him in the face, but prostrate on their knees and their elbows on the ground, with their hands open and joined above their heads, and

---

[1]   The story is a good one, but the historical records do not bear this out. Kosa Pan became Phra Klang or Barkalon to Petratcha after the fall of Phaulkon.

[2]   Bangri is marked on Walker's map of Siam (1828) on the west coast between Takuapa and Phuket.

their eyes fixed on the ground, or shut till he has passed by them; then they are permitted to rise and look on his back parts or side.

In the month of November he also shows himself on the river, in a ballon[1] or barge of thirty or forty yards long, about two yards broad, and two foot deep, with a throne placed near the middle of her length, about seven foot high, and a rich canopy over his head, and being seated on the throne, his greatest lords or minions sit under the throne, and about fifty or sixty rowers are seated afore and be-aft the throne (clothed in carnation-coloured waistcoats, with fine caps or turbans on their heads) to row or paddle His Majesty wherever he orders them, and there are ordinarily above 1,000 other barges to wait on His Majesty, besides several thousands of other common ballons, insomuch that for five or six miles the river is covered with boats, except near His Majesty's barge, and there is half a mile of the river clear for his barge to move in.

About four or five in the evening, he goes in his barge to a temple about three miles above the city[2], on the opposite side of the river, where the priests pray for him, and present him with two yards and an half of cotton cloth that must be spun and woven the same day that the king comes to receive it[3]. After sun sets, he embarks again (leaving some royal gratuity to the priests for their miraculous present) and is attended in state to his palace.

---

[1] The French term for the ceremonial Siamese barges.
[2] This temple is not identified.
[3] Hamilton seems to have got hold of the wrong end of the stick. The king would be presenting robes to the monks (in a *kathin* ceremony), not the other way round. The spinning and weaving is unlikely in practice to have been completed in one day.

His reason for honouring the river and his people that time of the year is to forbid the river formally to flow higher or longer than such a number of inches in height, or of days in time, as he sets it; yet sometimes it disobeys his royal commands[1].

All the mandarins belonging to the government whose affairs require their residence in the the city, whose numbers generally amount to 3,000, must daily attend in the palace, except they have leave to be absent, and if any one transgresses, he is severely whipped with split rattans, which cut pretty deep into the flesh, and leave conspicuous marks behind them[2]. The greater the marks appear, the greater the honour they take them to be. And the pretty ladies are not exeemed [sic] from the flagellation, for very small faults. And I have seen some pretty agreeable young gentlewomen with rattan marks on their backs, which they are so far from covering that as they pass the streets they expose their backs, though their breasts, bellies, and necks are covered with a scarf, seeming to glory in being so much taken notice of by the greatest king on earth.

The women in Siam are the only merchants in buying goods, and some of them trade very considerably. The husbands in general are maintained by the industry of their wives[3]. And the Europeans that trade to Siam accommodate themselves as they do in Pegu, with temporary wives, almost on the same conditions too, and it is thought

---

[1] The ceremony was known as 'the parting of the waters'.
[2] All agree on the severity of Siamese punishments at the time, but only Hamilton says people were proud of the marks they left, and consequently is suspect.
[3] Again, all contemporary commentators agree that Siamese women were industrious and maintained their husbands. Hamilton does not give the reason: the obligation of the menfolk to serve without pay their ruler for six months or more a year.

no disgrace to have had many temporary husbands, but rather an honour that they have been beloved by so many different men. The Christian priests cry down that way of marrying, and want every heretic, as well as Christian Catholic, to be tied to some young lasses of their bringing up, but the heretics, according to their innate principles, generally continue deaf and obstinate to the grave advice and sound doctrine of the holy fathers, and marry according to the Siam way. The Catholics dare not do so for fear of excommunication, but the Siam wives generally prove the most obedient, loving, and chaste, for which reason, when the Catholics once go from Siam to follow their business in other countries, they seldom return to Siam, but leave their beloved wives a legacy to the church, who is a very indulgent mother to her termagant[1] daughters.

The natives of both sexes go bare-headed, and their hair cut within two inches of the skin, and gummed, and combed upwards, which makes their head seem very big, and all in bristles like a boar's back. They are well-shaped in body and limbs, with a large forehead and a little nose, and handsome mouth with plump lips, and black sparkling eyes. Their ears of a moderate size, but large thick lappets. The men have but little hair on their chins, and they are of an olive colour, but the women [are] of a straw complexion, and some of the ladies have a little tincture of red in their cheeks and lips, but whether it is natural or artificial I know not. They are very prolific and long-lived, which may be partly imputed to their temperance in eating and drinking.

After the usurper had settled himself on the throne of Siam, he ordered the French to deliver their fort at Bangkok

---

[1] Here in its original sense of 'wandering', not its acquired meaning of 'shrewish'.

to an officer that he sent to take possession of it, but they refused, without first making terms for themselves; on which he sent a part of his army to attack it, and threatened every man's life that returned before it was taken. His orders were punctually put in execution, and all the French got was the honour of dying bravely in the defence of their liberty[1]. The fort stands still undemolished, but no artillery is in it.

In Siam they have several ways in punishing criminals with death, for theft and other suchlike peccadilloes.

---

[1]   As in nearly all elements relating to the anti-French, anti-Phaulkon coup in Siam of 1688, Hamilton is very wrong in having the French dying bravely in the defence of their liberty. General Desfarges withdrew from Lopburi to the incomplete fort in Bangkok on 5 June, which was defended by some 250 officers and men. The Siamese built some ten redouts; the fort on the opposite side of the river was abandoned by the French. Desfarges' two sons, taken hostage in Lopburi, were released. Negotiations began as rations ran low. The Bishop of Metellopolis, Mgr Laneau, was sent by Petratcha as an envoy. Kosa Pan, now Phra Klang, occupied the western fort and directed the blockade. It was agreed the French would withdraw on two frigates provided by the Siamese. The arrival of the French ship *Oriflamme* in September with more soldiers and guns changed the speed of the negotiations if not their outcome. The Bishop, Chevalier Desfarges (one of the French general's two sons) and Sieur Véret (the French factor) would stay as hostages until the frigates were returned. The remaining French garrison would leave, beating drums and carrying their impedimenta. The Siamese would provide provisions for one year against payment, Desfarges would restore the fort to a pristine condition. Once 'Mme Constance' had been disposed of (see p. 167 note 2), there were no further obstacles. The French withdrew on 2 November 1688. The three designated hostages accompanied the garrison to the bar of the Siam, where Véret and Chevalier Desfarges simply jumped bail and boarded the *Oriflamme*. After disputes over boatloads of supplies and the release of some Siamese hostages, the French set sail on 13 November for Pondichéry, leaving the luckless Bishop of Metellopolis with his priests and minute flock to face Siamese wrath.

Beheading is the common way. For rebellion or mutiny they are ripped up alive, and their guts and entrails taken out, and their carcasses woven up in a twig-case, and tied up to a stake for vultures and other voracious fowls or dogs to feed on. I saw eighteen one morning going to be executed so for mutiny. They were each put on a triangular seat, with their necks and hands in wooden fetters, and carried by three slaves in chains through the streets to the place of execution, but they looked as if they had been almost starved in prison, for they were very meagre. Some were weeping, others joyful that they were near the end of a miserable life.

For treason and murder, the elephant is the executioner. The condemned person is made fast to a stake driven into the ground for the purpose, and the elephant is brought to view him, and goes twice or thrice round him, and when the elephant's keeper speaks to the monstrous executioner, he twines his trunk round the person and stake, and pulling the stake from the ground with great violence, tosses the man and the stake into the air, and in coming down, receives him on his teeth, and shaking him off again, puts one of his forefeet on the carcass, and squeezes it flat.

In Anno 1717 the King of Siam made war on his neighbour of Cambodia, and invaded his country with an army of 50,000[1] by land, and 20,000 by sea, and committed

---

[1]   Wars between Siam and Cambodia were frequent; at this period Siam was pushing the claims to the throne of Thammoreachea (r.1702-3, 1706-10, 1738-47) against the Vietnamese-backed Ang Em (r.1699-1701, 1710-1722). There were major expeditions against the Cambodians in 1714 and 1722, but 1717 is not known to have been particularly bellicose, though Hamilton says below (p. 189 note 1) that the Siamese fleet destroyed the Cambodian port of Ponteamass in that year.

the care of his armies to his Barkalon, a Chinese[1] altogether unacquainted with war. The Chinaman accepted of the charge with much reluctancy, but the king would not be denied. The war proved unsuccessful, but I shall leave the particulars till I treat of Cambodia, and return to Siam, where I had some difficulties to meet with.

In Anno 1719 I went thither with a cargo to dispose on [*sic*], expecting to trade on the footing of the old treaty[2] concluded at London with the King of England and the King of Siam's ambassador in Anno 1684, but on my arrival, I found that Mr Collet, governor of Fort St George, had cancelled that agreement by his ambassador Powney[3], as I have already observed, and the new conditions being too hard for me to stand to, I solicited for liberty to depart again with my ship and cargo, which I could not obtain in less than four months.

[2]   Details are lacking about this person.
[2]   The treaty referred to did not exist. Hamilton was in Ayutthaya in 1718, not 1719.
[3]   On arriving in Ayuthaya to trade, Hamilton found himself forestalled by Captain John Powney, commanding a vessel in which Collet, the President of Madras, had financial interests. Hamilton assumed that a new treaty had been concluded between Siam and the Madras Presidency. All that was agreed were favourable terms concerning the duties to be paid by vessels hailing from Madras, and Siamese vessels trading with the Coromandel Coast were also granted favourable terms. But other traders were left to deal themselves with Siamese customs officials. Hamilton was told he had to pay 8% duty, 'measurage dues', and any return cargo must be bought from state officials. Hamilton found it impossible to trade with profit and after a delay of five months, he departed in December 1718, not in the best of tempers (Foster, I. xxxi). Letters passed between all sides; the Court of Directors in London in 1721 effectively censured both parties, allowing for free trade, and accommodating Hamilton. He however lost more than £3,000 in the affair.

Collet's attorney at the court of Siam was a Persian by birth[1], but had come to Siam with his father when very young, and had remained about forty years at Siam. He was as complete a rascal as Collet could have found for his villanous purposes, for by false informations [sic] to the king he had brought many honest men into trouble, and some treasure into the king's coffers.

When I understood that he was the remora[2] that had put a stop to my commerce, I tried if I could remove him by large presents, but all to no purpose, for if I traded, it must be on the scheme laid down by Collet, by the negotiation of Powney, who kept one Collison[3] as his resident at Siam, to consult and inform the Persian of the best methods to ruin the English traders that had not Collet's letters of protection.

This Persian (whose name was Oi-ya[4] Sennerat) and I were discoursing one day of my affairs in the Hindustan language, which is the established language spoken in the Mogul's large dominions, and, among other things, I was laying down to him the difficulties that might attend the King of Siam's trade carried on from Mergui to Fort St George, because if the rest of the English colonies were forbid trading with Siam, they had just cause to forbid his subjects to trade to Fort St George or anywhere else, and that other troubles might arise to the king's affairs, by thus imposing on the king, who was ignorant of the consequences that might follow in breaking the agreement

---

[1] There were many Persians in Siamese service, particularly before the rise to power of Phaulkon.

[2] Hindrance.

[3] James Collison was listed in 1717 as one of the 'seafaring men not constant inhabitants' at Madras.

[4] Sometimes Ok-ya, a Siamese title of nobility.

made in England without so much as once giving warning to the English colonies of other parts of India.

He answered me that the king of Fort St George could best give me an answer, who was able to protect the King of Siam's trade thither, and that His Majesty had no other foreign trade but Japan that he valued, and the English had no trade that way to disturb his master's commerce, and that if I did not comply with the agreement made by Powney in Collet's name, I might go away when I could.

I told him that I had a mind to see the king[1], and would make him[2] present of a 1,000 dollars if he could find means to introduce me to his presence. He answered me that the English had not good manners enough to be admitted into the presence of so great a king, and therefore I ought not to expect to appear before him, and, for fear I should have made application to some other court favourite to introduce me, about two or three days after our confabulation I heard that there was a proclamation published all over the city that no foreigner should dare to approach within such a distance of the king's palace, under very severe penalties.

About a week after I had a summons to appear before a tribunal to answer to an indictment of speaking treason of the king. I knew myself innocent, and appeared at the time appointed, which was about eight in the morning. The court was held in a large, square, oblong hall, open on all sides. About nine the judge came with some thousands of attendants, and, as he passed by me to take his place, he viewed me very narrowly, as I did him with much attention. He was a man of a middle stature, about fifty years of age, of a pleasant but grave countenance, and had a quick sparkling eye. He spoke to my interpreter to bid me have a care of my tongue, lest I should prejudice myself in

[1]   Phummintharacha (Thai Sa), r.1709-1733.
[2]   That is, Ok-ya Sennerat.

answering to intricate questions. I thanked him for his admonition, and told him "a word to the wise was sufficient".

Having placed himself, he ordered my indictment to be read, which was accordingly done, and in about half an hour's time it was ended. He asked me by my interpreter if I understood what was libelled against me. I answered no. He then bade the interpreter inform me of the meaning of each particular paragraph, as they were read a second time with deliberation, and, having heard my impeachment, which was grounded only on my saying "that the king had been imposed upon", I thought fit to deny all, and put my adversary Oi-ya Sennerat to prove that I had said so; but, by the by, I found that saying the King of Siam was capable of being imposed on is rank treason.

The judge chose out of the assembly two procurators for each of us, and there were no small debates for three or four hours, whether or not a stranger, who was ignorant of the laws of Siam, could come under the penalty annexed to the transgression of their laws, when they were broken through ignorance, and not with design; but my antagonist at last carried it in the affirmative, though the judge seemed to incline towards the opinions of my advocates.

Then the judge put Oi-ya Sennerat to prove what I was accused of, and he produced two of his own servants, who stood at some distance when we were discoursing of my affairs; but my advocates challenged the laws of Siam for their insufficiency, for that law admits not of a servant's testimony, either for or against his master. Then he proffered to bring an undeniable witness against me, who was the only person with us when we discoursed, and that was Collison, who was presently sent for, and being set by my adversary, the judge asked him by the interpreter if he was present at such a time when Oi-ya Sennerat and I were in warm discourse. He answered he was. He then interrogated him, if he had heard me say in my discourse that the king had been imposed on. He affirmed he had, on which I perceived a cloud overspread the judge's countenance, and many others who had come to hear the trial seemed sorrowful.

After a little pause, the judge, by the interpreter, asked me what I had to say to Collison's evidence. I answered that I had little knowledge of him, but that he might be an honest man or otherwise as his interest led him. All continued mute for a little space, and I broke the silence by desiring the judge to ask Collison in what language I held that discourse in with Oi-ya Sennerat, which the judge did, and was answered, that he did not well know, but that he believed it was in the Hindustan language. I begged the judge to ask him if he understood that language, and he did so. Collison, after some pause, answered, "No". Then the judge asked him angrily, and with an air of disdain, how he could come in as an evidence of words spoken in a language that he did not understand, and he simply said that he thought I had said so: at which the whole crowd gave an huzza, and clapped their hands and seemed joyful. The judge reprimanded Oi-ya Sennerat for putting him and the court to so much trouble, and complimented me on my safe delivery, and so departed seemingly well-satisfied[1].

I had two British gentlemen that accompanied me all the time of my trial. One was commander of a small ship from Bengal, called Mr Alexander Dalgleish[2], and one Mr John Saunders[3], who was second supercargo under me; and when the judge came, some executioners followed him with their instruments of death, to put the sentence in execution

---

[1]   Hamilton gives one of the most detailed accounts of Siamese justice involving foreigners at the time. He had little to complain of.
[2]   This seafarer is mentioned again a little later.
[3]   He was a 'free merchant' who became mayor of Madras in 1735.

as soon as the judge pronounces it. Our debates held so long that it was near eight at night before we got home. Had I been cast in my process, my head had been a sacrifice to my adversary's resentment, and my ship and cargo to the much injured king, and, to sum up all, my ship's company had been the king's slaves. On my returning home victorious, I had the congratulations of all my friends, particularly the Chinese merchants whose lives and estates might have been endangered by the like villanous informations.

My adversaries, being shamefully disappointed in that project, had one more to try their skill in, and that was to bring me in for piracy, for about four years before Mr Harrison[1], then governor of Fort St George, had sent a ship to Amoy in China, and some China merchants having taken goods and money, to the amount of 20,000 taels or £6,700 sterling; when the term of payment came, they eloped, and the supercargoes could have no redress, which made them give orders to the captain of the ship to make reprisals, which they did on a large junk belonging to the Barkalon of Siam, which junk they carried with them to Fort St George, and which fact my adversaries fixed on me, though at that time I was in Arabia or Persia, which I proffered to prove by some Muhammmadan merchants that saw me there; but all that I could allege would have been ineffectual, if I had not accidentally found some Chinese who belonged to the junk when she was seized, and who knew both me and Captain Jones[2], who was the captor, and so it never came to a trial.

It being high time for me to get from Siam at any rate, I applied myself to my judge for his assistance, and carried a

---

[1]   Edward Harrison was governor of Madras 1711-1717.
[2]   Little is known about this person, other than his trading through Amoy.

present of four yards of scarlet cloth, and some pieces of Surat goods, to the value of £20 in all. He received me very courteously, and promised me his assistance, but would accept none of my presents. At last, on my pressing him to take it, he accepted of the scarlet cloth, but would not touch any of the Surat goods, though they were very fine in their kind, but recommended me to two officers more, whom I must address to make my request be the easier granted, and he told me that those Surat goods would serve to make them my friends. I took his advice, and in three days had my clearance, for paying about £200 for my ship's measurage (an imposition of Mr Collet's) and so I fell down to Bangkok where, according to the Siam custom, I was obliged to put my guns ashore before I could go up to the city[1]. I lay there four or five days before orders were sent to deliver my guns, which, as soon as I had got on board and mounted, I told the officer that delivered them to give my service to Oi-ya Sennerat, and tell him that if the king's three junks arrived on this coast this season, he would hear further from me by them.

By that time I was clear at Bangkok, Captain Dalgleish arrived there also, in order to proceed to Bengal. He had fallen into the trap laid by Collet, and had paid measurage and customs, besides the usual presents to the court, according to the old constitution, but he could not get ready to go so soon out of the river as I, otherwise I designed to have brought some troubles on Sennerat, if not on Collet and Powney's affairs at Siam, but Captain Dalgleish being still in their power tied my hands.

Siam Bar is only a large bank of soft mud, and, at spring tides, not above ten or eleven foot water on it. It is easy getting into it in the southwest monsoons, because, in

[1]   Ayutthaya.

two or three tides, with the motion the ship receives from the small waves and the assistance of the wind, she slides through the mud. My ship drew thirteen foot, and we had not above nine on the bar when we went into the river, but coming out with the northeast monsoons, the sea being smooth, we are obliged to warp out[1] with anchors and hawsers[2] and, if the ship draws any considerable draught of water, we are sometimes two springs in warping over, but, at twelve foot draught, I got over in four tides.

And now, having given some particular accounts of my observations on and in Siam, I will also give some general remarks, and begin with the fertility of the country, which, on that point, is inferior to few (if any) in the world.

There are but two parcels of mountains to be seen in the places that I passed through, and they lie between east and northeast from the city of Odia, about ten leagues distant, and they produce good timber for building, and agala-wood for perfumes. They have also mines of iron, tin, lead, silver and gold, but they are all entailed on the crown, who has the sole benefit of them. They breed vast numbers of wild deer, which are hunted and killed for the sake of their skins, which they yearly send to Japan[3].

The plains produce all sorts of grain necessary for animal and human sustenance. They plentifully bear as good, if not the best oranges, lemons and limes in the world. Their rivers superabound in fish of several species, very good in their kind. Their villages are numerous, and well-inhabited with artificers[4] and peasants; but there are but five walled towns in all the Siam dominions, and Odia is one of them.

[1] To hand by ropes.
[2] Cables.
[3] This trade was a Dutch monopoly.
[4] Craftsmen.

They have abundance of wild animals in their woods, such as elephants, rhinoceroses, leopards and tigers, and tame cattle, as bullocks, buffaloes and swine in abundance about their farms. Temples and priests are more numerous here, in proportion to the laity, than in any country I ever saw out of the dominions of Portugal. Their tallapois or priests are distinguished from the laity by a cinnamon or orange-coloured cloak which they wear, they again differing among themselves by distinguishing badges by which they know their degree and dignity. Their heads, beards and eyebrows are kept close shaven. They are forbidden marriage or meddling with money, and if any of the priesthood is convicted of incontinency with women, he is burned for it alive, and, if only suspected and brought to a trial, he is degraded and banished.

They have sermons or lectures four times in a moon[1], the gates of the temples being set wide open, and the people meet in good order. Their sermons consist in recommending moral duties to the people, and charity towards one another, but particularly to the church, by which acts it subsists; and, after the priests' benediction, everyone goes to an image, and kisses it, or bows to it, and marches off in good order. They have morning and evening prayers, and sing anthems. They visit the sick, and pray for the dead, and accompany the corpse to the funeral pile, and sing obsequies. They go to weddings, and make sacrifices for the prosperity of the bridegroom and bride, but have no hand in joining them together.

Marriages are there made up by parents or near relations, without the consent of the parties to be married; for that reason they are commonly married very young. But if they are come to the years of discretion or maturity, then

---

[1]   On *wan phra* or holy days marking the phases of the moon.

the spark gets some female friend to acquaint his mistress with his passion for her, and if she will permit a visit from him the bargain is as good as made. The civil magistrate with them officiates the priest's part with us, and when once they are married, they seldom sue for a divorce, which is very hard to procure, except in case of insufficiency in the man, or barrenness in the woman, for adultery in either party is not reckoned infamous; and fornication is either allowed or tolerated.

The children are carefully educated in schools by priests set apart for that service, and it is rare to find a Siamese but who can write[1]. After schooling, they are put to such callings as suit best with their genius and quality; and there is generally a reciprocal harmony between parents and children. The children are obedient, and the parents indulgent. In childhood and youth the parent furnishes the child with what is necessary, and in old age the child supplies all the wants of his parent, as far as he is able. In marriages they make no account of consanguinity, further than between father and daughter, mother and son, and sister and brother; all other degrees are lawful.

And now it is time to steer my course to the southward again as far as Cambodia. Coasting alongshore, the first place we meet with is Ban Plasoi[2], a place not frequented by strangers, though it produces much agala and sappan-woods, and elephants' teeth; but all are sent to the king, who, for all his gaudy titles, yet stoops to play the merchant[3]. I suppose he makes use of trading in honour of

---

[1]   This was unusual elsewhere in Southeast Asia, and indeed in Europe at the time.

[2]   Now Chonburi; Hamilton writes 'Bangkasoy'.

[3]   The extension of royal trading privileges by King Narai led to a decline in the importance of Ayutthaya as a regional trading and entrepôt centre.

his kinsman Mercury[1], who superintends merchandising, but was never reckoned a fair dealer, and in that point the king is nearly related to him. But Ban Plasoi is famous chiefly for making *belacan*[2], a sauce made of dried shrimps, cod-pepper, salt and a seaweed or grass, all well mixed, and beaten up to the consistency of thick mustard. Its taste and smell are both ungrateful to the nose and palate; but many hundred tons are expended in Siam and the adjacent countries.

Ban Plasoi River[3] lies but four or five leagues to the eastward of Siam Bar, and there are two islands, called the Dutch Islands[4], where great ships are obliged to stay in the southwest monsoons when they cannot get water over the bar that bears off it southeast and by south, about nine leagues distant.

I observed before that the Company sent the *Herbert* and another ship from England in Anno 1685 and in 1686 as the *Herbert* lay at those islands, one Captain Udall, who commanded her, died[5] and the succeeding captain carried

---

[1] The Roman god of commerce, thieves, and eloquence, and messenger of the gods.

[2] The Malay term for the Siamese *kapi*, fermented shrimp paste. It is mentioned in the context of Pegu in Chapter One; see p. 19 note 3.

[3] Bang Pakong River.

[4] Ko Sichang. John Crawfurd, in his *Journal of an Embassy to the Courts of Siam and Cochin China* (London, 1828) and travelling between Bangkok and Vietnam, writes of "a group of islands close to hand, called by our old navigators the Dutch Islands, and by the natives Ko Si-chang." Hamilton's map incorrectly marks the islands Amsterdam; this was a Dutch store between Paknam and Bangkok on the Chao Phya.

[5] He was one of several foreigners who were killed in the Makassar uprising of 1686, which was put down by Phaulkon. Captain Udall's brother, Edmund, in a letter written to his wife from Ayutthaya circa October 1686, wrote, "Ashoare they would go. . . brother was immediately kild, his wounds being searcht (at the Dutch Factorey, where he was buried) by the Dutch doctor" (India Office Records: E/

his corpse ashore, and buried it in a pretty deep grave. Two days after, some of the ship's people going ashore had the curiosity to go and see the grave. When they came near, to their great wonder, they saw the corpse stripped of its winding sheet, and set upright against a tree. It was afterwards put again into the coffin, and buried in the same grave, with a quantity of heavy stones on it, and next day they came to the grave and found it opened a second time, with the corpse standing upright against another tree. So they made fast some stones to it, and carried it a pretty way into the sea, and buried it in the water, where it remained undisturbed. This strange resurrection left room for various conjectures, but the most probable seemed to be that some sorcerers took it up and put it in that posture, whilst they, by their sorceries or incantations, interrogated it about future events, and received answers through human organs. The matter of fact I have heard often affirmed by several who were there at the time and saw it, which made me enquire if any people in Siam used to enquire about future events after that manner, and I was told that they did.

The coasts of Liant[1] and Chantaburi[2] are the territories of Siam, but for fifty leagues and more along the seashore there are no seaports, the country being almost a desert. It produces good store of sappan- and agala-woods, with gum-lac and stick-lac, and many drugs that I know but little about.

3/46 no. 5574). The letter continues with a gory description of all his wounds. Whose body – if any – was buried on Ko Sichang is not known, but it was not Udall's.

[1]   Cape Liant (spelt by Hamilton Liampe in his text and Liam on his map), by modern Sattahip.

[2]   Sometimes called Chantaboon, which Hamilton spells Chiampo in his text. It is not marked on his map.

EAUWECK.
Hooft Stad van CAMBODE

The city of Lovek, from F. Valentyn, Oud en Nieuw Ludien 1724-6 Vol. 3.

CAMBODIA AND LAOS

G ives an account of Cambodia [and] its trade, also of a late war brought into their country by the Siamese, and the ill success they had

The first seaport to be met with is Kompong Som[1], a town in the dominions of Cambodia. It affords elephants' teeth, stick-lac and the gum gamboge[2] or cambodia; but there is no free commerce allowed there without a licence from the court of Cambodia.

The next place is Ponteamass[3], a place of pretty good trade for many years, having the conveniency of a pretty deep but narrow river, which, in the rainy seasons of the southwest monsoons, has communication with Bassac[4] or

---

[1] 'Cupangsoap' in Hamilton's text, recently rebaptized (and debaptized) Sihanoukville.

[2] A gum resin which derives its name from Cambodia.

[3] 'Pontaimas' is marked on J. Walker's map published in 1828 in J. Crawfurd, *Journal of an Embassy to the Court of Siam and Cochin China*. It is a little further inland from 'Kang-kaoor Hatian' and is linked to 'Panompeng' by a long canal, and to the Bassac branch of the Mekong by an unnamed stream. Modern maps mark Giangthanh in approximately the same position on the stream.

[4] The western arm of the Mekong delta.

Cambodia[1] River, which conveniency made it draw foreign commerce from the city of Cambodia[2] hither; for the city lying near 100 leagues up the river, and most part of the way a continual stream running downward, made the navigation to the city so long and troublesome that few cared to trade to it, for which reasons foreign commerce chose to come to Ponteamass, and it flourished pretty well till the year 1717 that the Siam fleet destroyed it.

When the Siam army and fleet threatened Cambodia, the king knew his inability to withstand the Siamese, so the inhabitants that lived on his borders had orders to remove towards the city of Cambodia, and what they could not bring with them, to destroy it, so that for fifty leagues the country was a mere desert. He then addressed the King of Cochin-China for assistance and protection, which he obtained, on condition that Cambodia should become tributary to Cochin-China, which was agreed to, and he had an army of 15,000 to assist him by land, and 3,000 in nimble galleys well-manned and equipped by sea.

The Siam army by land was above double the number of the Cambodians and Cochin-Chinese in conjunction, and their fleet above four times their number. The land army finding all the country desolate as they marched into the borders of Cambodia soon began to be in distress for want of provisions, which obliged them to kill their carriage beasts, and their elephants and horses which they could get no sustenance for, and the soldiers being obliged to eat their flesh. It being a diet they had never been used to, an epidemic flux and fever seized the whole army, so that in two months one half was not left, and those were obliged to

---

[1]   The Mekong.
[2]   Udong was the capital (slightly to the north of Phnom Penh) in the seventeenth century, and in the early eighteenth century it was moved to Lovek.

retreat towards their own country again, with the Cambodian army always at their heels.

Nor had their navy much better success, for they coming to Ponteamass sent in their small galleys to plunder and burn the town, which they did effectually[1], and, of elephants' teeth only, they burnt above 200 tons. The ships and junks of burden lying in the road above four miles from the town, the Cochin-Chinese taking hold of that opportunity, attacked the large vessels, and burned some, and forced others ashore, whilst their galleys were in a narrow river, and could not come to their assistance till high water that they could get out. The Cochin-Chinese having done what they came for, retired, not caring to engage such a superior number, and the Siamese fearing famine in their fleet steered their course for Siam with disgrace. In Anno 1720 I saw several of the wrecks, and the ruins of the town of Ponteamass.

The city of Cambodia stands on the side of the great river, about fifty or sixty leagues from Ponteamass by land, or by water in the southwest monsoons. The country produces gold of 21 carats fine, raw silk at 120 dollars per picul, elephants' teeth at 50 to 55 dollars for the largest. The small are of different prices. They have also much sappanwood, sandalwood, agala-wood, stick-lac[2], and many sorts of physical drugs, and lac for japanning. They are very desirous of having a trade with the English; but they will not suffer the Dutch to settle factories in their country[3].

---

[1] So effectively that the town disappeared without trace.

[2] Lac in its natural state on twigs, also mentioned in Chapter One and at the end of Chapter Twelve.

[3] The Dutch experience in Cambodia was not a happy one. A factory was established at Kampong Luong, near Udong in 1623, but the Muslim traders complained to the king's overseer, and all the Dutch

Provisions of flesh and fish are plentiful and cheap, and are the only things that may be bought without a permit from the king. I have bought a bullock that weighed between four and five hundredweight for a Spanish dollar; and rice is bought at 8 pence per pecul, which is about 140 lb., but poultry are scarce, because the country being for the most part woody, when the chickens grow big they go to the woods and shift for themselves. Tigers and wild elephants are numerous in the woods, and there are also wild cattle and buffaloes, and plenty of deer, all which animals everybody is free to catch or kill.

There are about two hundred topasses[1] or Indian Portuguese settled and married in Cambodia, and some of them have pretty good posts in the government, and live great after the fashion of that country; but they have no priests, nor will any venture to go among them, for in Anno 1710 a poor Capuchin went there to officiate, and finding one of the toppingest[2] of his congregation to have two wives, ordered him, by virtue of his sacerdotal power, to put one of them away, but his parishioner would not obey in that point, which made the priest use the weapon of excommunication against him, which the other took in such dudgeon that he knocked his spiritual guide's brains out for his unseasonable severity. Since that time they wrote to Siam and Macao in China for some more ghostly fathers, but not one will go, though perhaps they might have the honour of dying martyrs.

were massacred and their ships fired. Peace was finally made between the two in 1652.

[1] Topass, a Malayalam word from Hindi *dobashi*, meaning a man of two languages, hence an interpreter; in English, according to the *Shorter Oxford Dictionary*, "a dark-skinned half- breed of Portuguese descent; often applied to a soldier, or a ship's scavanger, or bath attendant, who is of this class".

[2] Most excellent.

They all of them have small pensions from the king, but too narrow to maintain them, so they go to the woods with firearms, and kill wild elephants for their teeth which they sell to foreigners; and their way of killing them is very singular, for they form a piece of iron like a slug[1], and the foremost end is made sharp. In the woods grow certain trees with a thick bark of a violent poisonous quality. They drive the sharp end of the slug into the bark, and let it stay a short time in it; then put the slug into their gun charged with powder, and coming near the beast, fire the slug into its body. The elephant being thus wounded, flees from the man, but the man keeps sight of it for a small space of time, and then it drops down dead.

And with the same poisoned slugs they kill cattle and buffaloes for their tongues. This subtle poison has also another strange quality, that if men become hungry or thirsty (as they often do in the woods) they squeeze a few drops of it on a leaf of a tree, and they licking the leaf, it gives immediate refreshment; but if the skin be broken, and the juice touch the part, it proves mortal without remedy.

When I arrived at Ponteamass, an officer came on board who could speak a little Portuguese. He brought a present of refreshments along with him, and advised me to send to the king, to give him an account of my arrival, and acquaint him that I designed to trade with his subjects by his permission, which I did, and in twelve days received an answer that I might, but desired me to send some person up with musters[2] of my goods, that he and his merchants might see them, and sent two Portuguese for interpreters, one to stay with me on board of my ship, while I stayed, and the other to accompany the person I designed to send to him with the musters. On their arrival I dispatched my

---

1 An irregular-shaped bullet.
2 Samples.

second supercargo, with an equipage of twenty-five men, well armed with fusees[1] and bayonets, with two small bales of musters and presents for the king, with instructions to let me hear from him once a week, by an express if no other opportunity offered.

After he arrived at the city, he had a large house allowed him for the accommodation of him and his retinue, and had a store of provisions sent him, and many folks of distinction visited him, but ten days passed before he could see His Majesty, who at last received him in great state, sitting on a throne like a pulpit[2], with his face veiled below his eyes, and after many gracious speeches, some whereof were pertinent to my purpose, but many not, he gave me liberty and encouragement to trade.

I had stayed above three weeks in expectation to hear from my second supercargo, but could get no account from him. I beginning to be uneasy, got an express to carry letters to him, and ordered him to send it back with as much speed as was possible, but had the mortification to find he had been stopped at the city. I was extremely uneasy for want of advice what was become of my people, and the approaching of the southwest monsoons, which would have made that coast a lee shore[3], and would have obliged me to take sanctuary in one of their harbours for five or six months, and was not certain whether I was in a friend's or an enemy's country. In this labyrinth I continued a week, and at last resolved to depart by a certain day, and leave my people to come after me to Malacca, if they were

[1] As on p. 84 note 1, light muskets or firelocks.
[2] In the same manner that the King of Siam received foreign envoys.
[3] The shore to the lee of a vessel (not the lee of the land), thus exposed. On a coast exposed to the southwest monsoon, Hamilton risked becoming embayed, trapped in a bay which he could not get out of until a change in wind direction occurred.

alive and at liberty. The goods I had sent up with them would have been sufficient to have hired a vessel to carry them thither. I told my resolution to my interpreter, and that I should be obliged to carry him and some more of the king's subjects along with me as hostages for the civil treatment of my people at Cambodia. He seemed surprised at my resolution, and got a person to go to the city in all haste to give an account of my impatience and design, who returned in fourteen days, about two days before my term was expired that I had set for my departure. There accompanied him three Portuguese, who brought me letters from my second supercargo, that he had taken leave of the king, and was coming to me with all haste, and in three days after the Portuguese came he arrived with all his retinue, with a letter of compliment to me in the Portuguese language, and one directed to the governor of Bombay, to invite the English to settle in his country and to build factories or forts in any part of his dominions to protect trade.

The reason why he kept us so long in suspense was that he would enter into no correspondence with us without the knowledge and consent of his guardian the King of Cochin-China[1], who at last consented to allow us commerce both in Cambodia and in his own proper dominions, but that the Siamese had destroyed the country where they had been, and they had nothing ready for barter with my cargo then, but in a year or two they would be provided.

When the king bestows his favour on any person whom he has a mind to honour, which he never does without a considerable present, he presents the person with two

---

[1]   Le Du-Ton (Hoa Houang-De), r.1705- 1729. Cambodia owed dual allegiance, to both Cochin-China and Siam, and was frequently torn between the two.

swords to be carried always before him when he goes abroad in public; one is the sword of state, and the other of justice. All people that meet him when those swords are carried before him must give him place, and salute him by a set form of words, but if he meets with another court minion, then they compare the dates of their patents, and seniority takes place, and must be first saluted. Wherever those mandarins go in the country, they hold courts of justice, both civil and criminal, and they have the power of laying on fines, but they are paid into the king's treasury; but in capital crimes, his sentence is law, and speedy execution follows sentence.

The Cambodians are of a light brown complexion, and very well shaped, their hair long, and beards thin. Their women are very handsome, but not very modest. The men wear a vestment like our nightgowns, but nothing on their heads or feet. The women wear a petticoat reaching below the ankle, and on their bodies a frock made close and meet for their bodies and arms, and both sexes dress their hair.

I saw none of their priests, but understood from my interpreter that they worship the same gods that are adored in Siam. They worship the great god under the name of Tipedah, and Phra Prumb, and Phra Put[1], are his sons. The church subsists by freewill offerings, and their priests are not much respected, being generally chosen from among the lower sort of the laity.

The kingdom of Laos borders on Siam, Cambodia, Cochin-China, and Tonkin. It produces gold, raw silk, and elephants' teeth are so plentiful that they stake their fields and gardens about with them to keep out wild hogs and cattle from destroying their fruit and corn. They are all pagans in religion.

---

[1]   See p. 152 notes 1-2 to Chapter Twelve.

The natives of Laos are whiter in complexion than their circumjacent neighbours. I saw some of them at Siam, of both sexes. Their women were little inferior to Portuguese or Spanish ladies.

There are several islands that lie off the coast of Cambodia, but none are inhabited, because the saleiters or pirates that infest that coast rob them of what they get by pains and industry, though there is one about three leagues west of Ponteamass, called Quadrol[1] that has good qualifications for a settlement. It is about three leagues long, and one broad. Wood and fresh water are plentiful, the ground of a moderate height, the soil black and fat, except along the east side which faces Ponteamass, and that has several fine sandy bays, and they are good safe harbours in the rainy and windy seasons.

About thirty leagues east-south-east from Ponteamass is the west entrance of Cambodia River, generally called Bocca de Carangera[2]. The shallowest place in the channel in going in is four fathoms, and within it deepens to twenty in some places. The north entrance is broader, but much shallower, and lies about ten leagues distant from the west channel, but is little frequented. Between Ponteamass and the river are several small uninhabited islands. Pulau Panjang[3] is the largest, and consists of a cluster of eight islands, which form a pretty good harbour. Pulau Obi[4] is the eastmost, and affords good masts for shipping.

Pulau Condore[5] is the largest and highest, composed of four or five islands. It lies about fifteen leagues south of the

---

[1]   Possibly Phuquoc.
[2]   Camao Point.
[3]   The island is a considerable way from the coast.
[4]   South of Camao Point.
[5]   Con Son Islands, some 80 km from the coast. Most of the English settlers on the island were murdered on 2 March 1705 in an uprising

west channel of Cambodia River. Pulau Condore had once the honour of an English colony settled on it, by Mr Allan Catchpole[1], in Anno 1702 when the factory of Chusan, on the coast of China, was broke up, he being then director for affairs of the English East India Company in those parts.

He made a bad choice of a place for a colony, that island producing nothing but wood, water, and fish for catching. He got some Makassars to serve for soldiers, and help to build a fortification, and made a firm contract with them to discharge them at the end of three years if they were minded to quit his service, but did not perform what was contracted, which was the cause of his own ruin, and the loss of the colony, for those eastern desperadoes are very faithful where contracts and covenants are duly observed when made with them, but in defaillance[2], they are revengeful and cruel. Mr Catchpole having detained the Makassars beyond their time of agreement, still entrusted them with the guard of his own person and the garrison, and they taking the opportunity of the night, when all the English were in their beds who lodged in the fort, they inhumanely murdered them all. There was some noise made by those who were awake, which a few who lodged without the fort hearing took the alarm, and ran to the seaside, where kind providence directed them to a boat ready fitted with oars and sail, which they embarked in, and put off from the shore, and were not a stone's throw off till the bloody villains on the shore were in quest of them. So those in the boat, with much fatigue, hunger, and thirst

of indentured Makassarese. The islands became a penal settlement under the French.

[1] Allan Catchpole went under EIC auspices to Chushan, near Ningpo in China in 1699, removed to Condore in 1703, and was murdered there in 1705.

[2] In default.

in sailing and rowing above 100 leagues, got to some place of the King of Johor's dominions, where they were treated with humanity. The reverend and ingenious Doctor Pound[1], was one of those that escaped, and Mr Solomon Lloyd[2], an old acquaintance of mine, was another.

There were two harbours, or anchoring places, at Pulau Condore, but neither of them good. One at the northeast end they were forced to use in the southwest monsoons, the other on the west side for the northeast winds, the bottom of which is rocky, and therefore dangerous for losing anchors and cables, yet that was the place chosen to build their fort on, but since a factory was thought necessary to be settled on that coast, I wonder why they chose these islands, rather than Quadrole which I mentioned before.

The city of Cambodia is reckoned to lie 100 leagues up from the bar, and the river filled with low islands and sandbanks. The country of Laos is about forty leagues farther up, but what navigation is used above the city of Cambodia is done by small rowing vessels, and the river being one of the longest in the world[3] employs great numbers of those rowing boats.

---

[1] The Rev. James Pound had gone to China in 1699 with Catchpole as chaplain but was in Cambodia at the time of the Condore massacre; he returned to England in 1706.

[2] He was sent to China with Catchpole and knew Chinese; he did not in fact escape the massacre, according to Foster.

[3] Hamilton is correct in this, though little was known about the upper Mekong for another 150 years. The Mekong is 4,184 km long.

Ordinary mode of conveyance of persons of rank in Cochin-China,
from John Crawfurd, Journal of an Embassy to the Courts of Siam and Cochin-China 1828.

COCHIN-CHINA AND TONKIN

Treats of Cochin-China, and Tonkin, their religion, laws, and customs

Cochin-China is only divided from Cambodia by the river, which in some places is three leagues broad. It is a country far larger than Cambodia, and much richer, and the inhabitants more courageous and hardier for enduring fatigues in labour or war than the Cambodians, but are not so conversable and civil to strangers. The Cochin-Chinese draw one half of the customs and taxes raised in Cambodia by commerce and merchandising, but they give little encouragement for strangers to trade with them. Their country abounding in gold, raw silk, and drugs, they bring them to Cambodia to dispose of there, except what they send yearly to Canton in China; and I have seen some of their junks trading at Johor and Batavia.

Their religion is pagan after the China way, worshipping the same gods after the same manner as the Chinese do. Their laws are severe and bloody for crimes of treason, for not only the guilty person suffers a painful death, but the relations within the bounds of consanguinity suffer death also. Their cities and towns are divided into wardships, and at the ends of each street are railed gates, placed to confine each ward within its own limits. These gates are shut and locked every night, so that they have no communication by night, but if a fire breaks out in one of the wards, its whole inhabitants are cut off except the women and children.

There are but few Christians tolerated in Cochin-China, yet there was (and perhaps is) a French priest in great esteem among them, but it is capital for any other priest to be found in their country. This Frenchman kept a correspondence by writing with Mr de Cissé, Bishop of Siam, and he having a relation of the danger Christian priests were in there, made the old zealot half-mad to get thither, to receive the honour of martyrdom, and had he been honest in his promises to me (which was only not to protect any of my fugitive seamen at Siam[1]) I would have favoured him with a passage to Cambodia, from whence he might have easily gone to get that glorious crown[2].

Cochin-China has a large seacoast of about 700 miles in extent, from the River of Cambodia, to that of Quambin[3], and it has the conveniency of many good harbours on it, though they are not frequented by strangers; and along the east coast it is very deep, for in several places I sounded the depth, and found between sixty and eighty fathoms within half a league of the shore.

There are several islands on this coast. Those nearest the shore are not dangerous. Pulau Cecir de Terre[4] lies most

[1] See Chapter Twelve, p. 155 note 4.
[2] Hamilton had little patience any religious excesses. The cause of his dispute with Mr de Cissé is found on p. 156.
[3] Foster identifies this as the Fragrant River, at Hué. Mendes Pinto speaks, somewhat confusingly, of "a river called Pulo Cambin which divides the domain of Cambodia from the Kingdom of Champa at latitude nine degrees." By Hamilton's days Champa had been entirely extinguished.
[4] Kulao Kau.

southerly, and nearest the shore. It is uninhabited, and looks only like a parcel of scorched rocks, without either tree, bush, or grass to be seen on it. I passed within a mile of it, and it lies about a mile from the shore. Pulau Cecir de Mer[1] and all the chain of islands that stretch from the dangerous shallows of Paracel[2] are rather to be accounted rocks than islands. Pulau Cambir[3] lies about fifteen leagues off the shore, near the Paracels. It is uninhabited though pretty large. Pulau Canton[4] lies near the shore, and so do the islands of Champello[5], but there are no dangers lie off from them. There are strong currents that run to the southward in the northeast monsoons, which makes pilots take care to keep near the Cochin-China coast for fear of being driven among the Paracels, which are a dangerous chain of rocks, about 130 leagues long, and about fifteen broad, and have only some islands at each end. There are several inter-currents among those rocks, but no known marks to keep clear of dangers by, yet I knew an English ship from Surat that drove accidentally through them, and neither knew nor saw their danger till it was over, when they unexpectedly saw the coast of Cochin-China.

In Anno 1690 a Portuguese ship was lost on one of the northernmost islands of the Paracels, and all were lost but three or four persons who swimmed ashore. There were many pieces of the wreck followed them, and some cannisters of flour were accidentally thrown ashore,

[1] Co Loo Hon, some 250 km directly east of modern Saigon.
[2] A group of islands southeast of Hainan.
[3] Gambir. Mendes Pinto's Pulo Cambin, which appears as such in Walker's 1828 map, opposite 'Port Coumong.'
[4] Rai. Walker marks this as Callao Ray, placing it northeast of Cape Bantangan.
[5] Cham, off the coast south of Da Nang. It is called Pulo Champeilo by Mendes Pinto and is marked on Walker's 1828 map as Cham Callao, off the mouth of the river leading to Faiso.

whereby they were supported. They built an hut of what timbers and boards they could use for that purpose, and they found some fresh water in the caverns of the rocks, and in one place they built a cistern to save the rain water for the dry season. They took seaweeds and mixed with mud that they found about the coast of the island, and placing that mixture in a convenient part to retain the rain water, they subsisted by that means a dry season. Their food was sea fowls and tortoises which frequented that island in great numbers. In three years they all died but one, and in Anno 1701 a ship bound to Macao, coming near the island against their will, seeing the figure of a man waving his hands over his head, they had compassion and sent their boat to the island, and were astonished to find the person to be one of their own countrymen, and much more when he told them his misfortunes, and how long he had been alone on that island. They clothed him and fed him, and carried him to Macao, where I saw him in Anno 1703, and had the account from his own mouth.

But it is time to return back to Cochin-China, which about three or four centuries ago[1] was but a province of Tonkin; at least they were both under the dominion of one king, who, dying without issue, divided the government of his dominions between a brother and a sister of his, whom he very much esteemed for their good qualities. He ordered his brother to reside in Cochin-China, and take care of affairs there, while the sister took care of the government of

---

[1] The first separation of Tonkin and Cochin-China seems to have occurred under Le Loi in 1428, who fought against the Tran dynasty in Tonkin. War was endemic between the two; a particularly difficult moment was in 1627 when Trinh Trang, the ruler of Tonkin invaded Cochin-China and Nguyen Sai-Vong repulsed him. There were further unsuccessful attempts at invasion in 1643, 1648, 1659, 1661, and 1672.

Tonkin, but to have a meeting once a year to consider and consult of matters for the good of the state.

The lady being young thought fit to marry, and the harmony of state soon ended by the marriage. The husband grew ambitious, and wanted the government wholly in his own hands, but carried fair with his brother-in-law, and one time talking with the queen of the necessity of uniting both kindoms into one, as formerly, and that of right both belonged to her, as being possessed of the most ancient and noble kingdom, and that in order to get both kingdoms into her hands, he would find a way to cut off her brother, without suspicion of their being accessory to it. The queen, seeming to approve of the design, privately let her brother know his danger; being then at the court of Tonkin, she advised him to pretend to go hunting for a few days, but to make what haste he could unto his own government, where he might be secure from conspiracies on his life, which advice he followed, and got safe into Cochin-China, and calling a council of his nobles, related the whole affair to them.

The Cochin-Chinese took the designed injury to their prince so ill that from that time they renounced all friendship and commerce with the Tonkinese, and the River Quambin being made the bounds of Tonkin dominions to the southward, and of Cochin-China to the northward, they both raised armies of forty or fifty thousand men each, and they continue still facing one another, the river lying between them, and nothing of action has happened all this while. If any Cochin-Chinese happens to flee from the justice of his own country to the Tonkiners, they receive him kindly, and treat him civilly, but if a Tonkiner fall under the same circumstances, and go for sanctuary to the Cochin-Chinese, he is condemned to slavery, and so must continue till he gets a pardon from his own court, and pay his ransom.

Tonkin is the next kingdom I must steer to of course, where the English and Dutch both had their factories, but the English Company's affairs being a little out of order, they withdrew theirs in January 1698 and the Dutch finding but little advantage by their trade in Tonkin, withdrew theirs about six years after[1]. However, the English had a private trade pretty good till the year 1719 that an English ship from Bengal ruined it by an act of violence.

The ship being laden and ready to sail, fell down the river from Kechio[2], the capital city of Tonkin, and in defiance to the known laws of the country, the supercargo got a Tonkin girl on board, in order to carry her with him; but her friends missing her, informed the civil magistrate, who sent to demand her, but the supercargo would not resign his mistress, whereupon acts of hostility ensued, and some were killed on both sides, and Captain Wallace[3] who commanded the ship had the fortune [sic] to be one of the slain. However, the English bravely carried off their prize, but I never heard any more of the Tonkin trade since.

Tonkin is bounded with Cochin-China on the south, Laos on the west, Kwangsi[4] a province of China on the north, and the ocean on the east. The country is prodigiously fruitful in all things necessary for the conveniency and support of life.

It produces gold and copper, but neither of them fine. They have abundance of raw silk, and manufacture part of it in wrought silks, but none fine. Their baaz[5] is the best, which they generally dye black. It wears very long, because

[1]   The Dutch had a factory in Tonkin from 1637 to 1700.
[2]   Ke-sho or Kecio, the old name for Hanoi.
[3]   Richard Wallace, captain of the Success, died circa 1721.
[4]   The southernmost province of China, between Yunnan and Kwantung.
[5]   Perhaps from Chinese pai-sze, white silk.

204

it is soft and well spun, and the oftener it is washed, the colour looks brighter, if blacker may be so called. They make bowls, cups, and tables, of rattans, and cover them very neatly with lac of divers colours, and gild them. They have also some porcelain[1] but very coarse and ill-painted. And those are the commodities for exportation from Tonkin.

There is a great chain of impassable mountains that run from the sea above 150 leagues, along the confines of Kwangsi and Kweichow[2], provinces of China, which secure Tonkin from any invasions that may come that way from China, and those mountains are covered with thick woods well stocked with wild elephants, tigers, and deer, but the use or ostentation of training up tame elephants is not much minded in Tonkin, nor in China.

The Christian religion is strictly forbidden to be preached in Tonkin, yet there are some Christians of the Romish church there[3]. Their own religion is pagan according to the doctrine of China. And they have a tradition, that many ages ago, Tonkin and Cochin-China and were both provinces of China[4].

The Tonkiners used to be very desirous of having a brood of Europeans in their country, for which reason the greatest nobles thought it no shame or disgrace to marry their daughters to English and Dutch seamen for the time they were to stay in Tonkin, and often presented their sons-in-law pretty handsomely at their departure, especially if they left their wives with child, but adultery was dangerous

---

[1]   An interesting reference to Vietnamese blue-and-white.
[2]   To the north of Kwangsi.
[3]   Missionary activity, especially French, was marked from the seventeenth century.
[4]   Vietnam was under Chinese rule from 111 B.C. to 939 A.D., apart from two brief insurrections in the sixth and early seventh centuries.

to the husband, for they are well versed in the art of poisoning.

The men and women are both well-shaped, and tolerably beautiful, but of a low stature. The maids keep their teeth very white, till they have lost the blue of their plumb[1], and then they dye them as black as jet, with the juice of a certain herb which they hold in their mouths for three days successively, and the black tincture continues ever after; but while that juice is in their mouths, they dare not swallow their spittle, it being of a poisonous quality.

---

[1] The phrase, mentioned in the *Oxford English Dictionary*, which cites Hamilton, clearly means the bloom of their freshness; it may mean rather more, and refer to losing their virginity.